KETO
LIVING 3 COLOR
COOKBOOK

COPYRIGHT

DISCLAIMER

Before we get started, a quick note on the nutritional information found at the bottom of each recipe.

Simply put, I've done my best to fastidiously calculate the macro nutrient breakdown, however obviously there will be variations in everyone's exact kitchen creation, due mainly to brand choices, different cuts of meats etc.

So please, understand that as a general rule they should be fairly close in the calculations, and are included primarily to serve as a beneficial guide to keeping you on track.

And as an FYI, the net carb count has been calculated by deducting the dietary fiber from the total carbohydrates.

I certainly hope that the info proves useful and accurate to you, and of course if you wish to double check my calculations on any recipe, I would always recommend that you please do so if you feel the need.

Next, in regard to the photographs, although most of your completed cooking efforts will closely match the image depicted alongside the recipe, due to various reasons, (creative and otherwise), some images shown may vary slightly in serving size, garnish, or contain other minor variations in look or style in comparison to your own finished creation.

Lastly, (and really just as a standard requirement for cookbooks that support a certain dietary path), regardless of any successes and goals I have personally achieved on a Keto lifestyle, it needs to be said that it is up to the individual to consult with their own medical professional to ensure that any changes to your diet are suited to you, and in saying so, the publisher and author carries no liability in a readers choice to follow a Ketogenic diet, and by extension, the preparation and consumption of any of the recipes contained herein this book.

KETO LIVING3 COLOR

COOKBOOK

LOSE WEIGHT WITH 101 ALL NEW DELICIOUS & LOW CARB KETOGENIC RECIPES

BY **ELLA COLEMAN** & NIGEL BURLINGTON

THE
KETO COURSES

FOREWORD

Welcome to Keto Living 3!

The first two Keto Living Cookbooks were so much fun to create.

For so many of us, Keto is significantly more than just a selection of our favorite recipes. I know that for me personally, it's a way of life, and in many ways, Keto has saved my life.

More and more the low carb movement is gaining traction, as people learn about insulin response and the mechanisms of fat storage in greater detail. And slowly the benefit of not only low carb eating, but increased fats in a diet is also becoming known.

What we have here is not only an extremely effective way to lose weight and regain lost health, but a diet that contains an outstanding array of delicious choices.

We live in a time where a little bit of sugar substitute science combined with some carefully constructed dishes, and a touch of love and effort can transform our lives from fat storage machines into ketogenic fat burning furnaces, without sacrificing taste or happiness.

Combined with a burst of well-intentioned exercise here and there (easier to do as the weight comes off), living Keto makes goals into reality every day, and really is a no brainer.

Regardless of education, it's worth a reminder that one of the most important components of success in just about any venture in life, is support, so on that note I just want to give a shoutout here before we begin to one of the most active and supportive Keto communities to be found.

Especially good for those starting out in Keto and not sure where to commence, I strongly recommend the very helpful, supportive and active community at these reddit.com subreddits:-

www.reddit.com/r/keto

www.reddit.com/r/ketorecipes

Once there, enjoy the 100's of success stories, tips, and community contributed recipes they have to offer. It really is a very welcoming and sharing site full of great information and people, and it's useful for not only new comers but also those seasoned in the art of Keto Living.

Frequenting supportive communities such as these, and armed with a couple of good recipe books in hand, you're well on the road to achieving your goals.

Now let's dive in to 101 new Keto creations.

After my first two books, I received a lot of requests for photos to go alongside the recipes.

Well, always up for a challenge, I contacted my good friend and food photographer, Alex Moss, and with the help of industry respected chef, Nigel Burlington, and editor, Gill Van Rooyen we got to work on what became a fantastic experience for all involved, with a great deal of laughter and yes... a few too many tastings along the way.

The 1st Keto Living book took us on a journey through all of the courses, breakfasts, mains, and desserts.

The 2nd Keto Living book was a cornucopia of savory and sweet snack sensations, a delicious assault on the senses designed to debunk the myth that living Keto meant living boring.

This 3rd book is designed to offer the perfect and balanced number of dishes and variety for every course of the day that will keep you cooking amazing Keto goodies for all hours of the day for many moons to come.

And, as with all the Keto Living books, each recipe is replete with nutritional info and net carbohydrate count per serve, to help you stay informed and keep your journey on course.

Reaching your goals is easy with the right tools!

I'm ecstatic to share this all new selection of recipes to accompany you on your journey, and I'm humbled by the positive response I have received from so many people.

I'm sure you'll love this cookbook in the Keto Living series as much as I have enjoyed preparing it.

Now let us travel together, side by side, Keto Living!

ADDITIONAL CONTRIBUTORS

NIGEL BURLINGTON
SOUS CHEF

Australian, Nigel Burlington has been a well-respected industry chef for two decades, with a particular specialty in pastries.

His ability to keep a kitchen calm under pressure while continually working to assist with the creation and preparation of a stream of perfectly plated courses, is an art form in itself.

His input and assistance in the kitchen is invaluable. Any dish Nigel cooks benefits significantly from his strict attention to detail, quality and love of food and not only tastes amazing, but also has a truly world class presentation.

ALEX MOSS
PHOTOGRAPHY & GRAPHIC DESIGN

Alex Moss, photographer and design professional, contributed his decades of experience, his love of a Keto lifestyle and creative skill behind the lens to deliver stunning image after image.

As each plate left the kitchen, Alex's photography managed to lift Keto Living 3 from simple food on a plate into a display of desirable mouth-watering beauty.

Also a designer, Alex set the graphic design of the printed book.

GILL VAN ROOYEN
EDITOR

Gill has been involved in cooking and editing cookbooks for many years. Her interest lies in cooking styles and ingredients available in different countries around the world as well as requirements for specific diets, with a particular interest in Keto.

Her ability to edit, tweak sentences, and assist with formatting documents and recipe editing makes her a powerful asset.

A NOTE ON SUGAR SUBSTITUTES

The second book in this series, 'Keto Living 2: Lose Weight with 101 Yummy & Low Carb Ketogenic Savory and Sweet Snacks', includes an informative section on types of sugar substitutes.

This was of course necessary due to the large amount of scrumptious sweet snack recipes that lay within!

For those who don't own Keto Living 2 yet, let me give you a concise version here of what you could do when you encounter recipes that call for sugar substitutes in this book.

In cases where a recipe calls for a **granulated or powdered sugar substitute**, we are looking to use a product that is for all intents and purposes a cup for cup exchange of product by volume, using a granular blend for granular, and powdered for powdered.

In all nutritional panels this has been calculated and added to the totals as if the increasingly popular sweet polyol (or sugar alcohol), Erythritol was used, and this has been calculated at 0.2 carb calories per gram.

Erythritol, when used in direct replacement for sugar is 70% as sweet as sugar and a very nice low carb, low GI ingredient to use that is also dental friendly with minimal complaints of stomach upset at consumption levels of under 50g of product per day.

If the 70% sweetness doesn't quite meet the grade, a couple more tablespoons (per cup) can make it up without altering the structure of most recipes, or better still, blending in a couple of drops of a liquid sweetener of your choice such as Stevia or Sucralose can add a nice synergy to the flavor.

You'll want to avoid granular sugar substitutes that include Maltodextrin or Dextrose as a filler, as the GI and caloric content is actually very similar to sugar. Also avoid falling for packaging claims of zero calories that may not be telling the whole story.

Now, in the case a recipe calls for a **liquid sugar substitute**, I have kept things simple, and simply recommended liquid Stevia.

With liquid Stevia, sweetness intensity can vary from brand to brand depending on the actual percentage of steviol content added to the product (purer is better).

Without getting too technical, there is also variety in taste and bitterness of Stevia depending on whether the steviol extracted from the plant is Stevioside or the less bitter, and 50% sweeter Rebaudioside A (which I prefer), and this isn't always marked clearly on the label.

Also, if you choose something else like Sucralose as your preferred liquid sweetener, you'll need to adjust the quantity used, as the sweetness of Sucralose is about double that of Stevia.

Aside from the above, feel free to experiment with the many options out there as different substitutes yield different results in the final product, in more ways than one.

There is more information to be found in Keto Living 2 on this subject, but for now, this will help you enjoy creating the recipes contained within this book.

And remember, when it comes to sweetness, if in doubt, a taste test is usually the best practice!

BREAKFAST

BREAKFAST CHEESY PANCAKES

Pancakes are always a special treat for breakfast and these are no exception. Serve with sugar free syrup or sandwich them around crispy bacon slices.

Serves 4

DIRECTIONS

In a small bowl mix together well the egg yolks, cream cheese, mozzarella and cream.

Season with salt and pepper.

In a separate bowl, whisk the egg whites until they form soft peaks.

Fold the egg whites carefully into the cheese mixture.

Melt the butter in a non-stick skillet over a medium heat and add the oil.

Using a soup ladle or a large serve spoon, place approximately one eighth of the batter into the skillet.

Cook gently until brown on the base.

Carefully flip over and brown the other side.

Remove the pancake when cooked and keep warm in a kitchen towel whilst the others are cooking.

If your skillet is large enough cook a few at a time.

Serve and enjoy!

INGREDIENTS

2 **large fresh eggs**, separated

4 ounces (113g) **cream cheese**

1 tbsp. **heavy cream**

1 tbsp. **grated mozzarella cheese**

1 tbsp. **olive oil**

1 tbsp. **butter**

Salt and pepper to season

NUTRITONAL FACTS
per pancake

Calories 208, Fat 20.5g, Carbohydrate 1.1g, Dietary Fiber 0g, Net Carbs 1.1g, Protein 5.9g

NUTTY BREAKFAST MUFFINS

Makes 8

DIRECTIONS

Preheat the oven to 350°F (177°C).

Line 8 muffin cups with paper muffin cases.

In a medium sized bowl, thoroughly mix together the almond flour, flaxseed meal, baking powder, baking soda, cinnamon and salt.

Add the coconut and sugar substitute.

In a separate bowl, mix together the melted butter, vanilla, cream and water.

Beat into the eggs.

Add this liquid mixture to the dry ingredients and mix well together.

Spoon this mixture evenly among the muffin cups.

Bake for 18 – 20 minutes until brown and the mixture is cooked. Test with a toothpick if necessary.

Cook for a few minutes longer if needed.

Remove from the oven and cook on a cake rack for a few minutes before removing the muffins from the cups.

NUTRITONAL FACTS
per muffin

Calories 306, Fat 25.9g, Carbohydrate 9.2g, Dietary Fiber 5.2g, Net Carbs 4.0g, Protein 8.4g

Muffins for breakfast – yum! These muffins may be frozen and reheated in the microwave for an easy breakfast option. Use almond extract instead of vanilla if you prefer. Top with some chopped macadamias if you like.

INGREDIENTS

1⅓ cups (128g) **fine almond flour**

⅔ cup (74g) **fine flaxseed meal**

¾ tsp. **baking powder**

1 tsp. **powdered cinnamon**

½ tsp. **baking soda**

¼ tsp. **salt**

¾ cup (70g) **unsweetened coconut**

1¼ cups (250g) **granulated sugar substitute**

2½ ounces (71g) **butter**, melted

1½ tsp **vanilla extract**

3 tbsp. **heavy cream**

2½ tbsp. **water**

2 **large fresh farm eggs**, beaten

ASPARAGUS, CHEESE & BACON OMELET

These are individual breakfast serves but the omelet could also be made in a larger dish for slicing and serve. Substitute the bacon for ham or even pepperoni if you wish. Different herbs will give a different flavor. It is up to you!

INGREDIENTS

12 **small spears fresh asparagus**, lightly cooked

1 tsp. **fresh parsley**, chopped

2 **rashers bacon**, fried until cooked

1 **green onion**, finely sliced

¼ **green bell pepper**, seeded and finely chopped

1 clove **garlic**, finely chopped

¼ cup (27g) **Gruyere cheese**, grated

2 tbsp. **unsweetened almond milk**

¼ tsp. **whole grain mustard**

2 large **fresh eggs**

½ tbsp. **olive oil**

½ tbsp. **butter**

Salt and pepper to season

Makes 2

DIRECTIONS

Trim the asparagus spears and cut in half.

Heat the oil in a medium sized skillet over a medium high heat.

Gently sauté the green onions, bell pepper and garlic in the skillet until tender but not browned.

In a bowl whisk the eggs.

Stir in the milk, Gruyere cheese, mustard and parsley.

Add the sautéed vegetables.

Heat half of the butter in a small omelet pan over a medium high heat.

Pour half of the egg mixture into the hot pan.

Cook until the omelet is done, lifting the sides as it cooks to allow the liquid egg to run underneath.

Place half of the bacon and the asparagus on one side of the omelet.

Turn one side over the other and serve.

Repeat with the other half of the mixture.

Serve hot.

NUTRITONAL FACTS
per serve

Calories 348, Fat 25.5g, Carbohydrate 8.4g, Dietary Fiber 3.6g, Net Carbs 4.8g, Protein 24.0g

HAM & MUSHROOM CUPS

Makes 6

DIRECTIONS

Preheat the oven to 375°F (191°C).

Lightly grease 8 muffin cups.

Line the muffin cups with the ham slices, they will flute up the sides.

Place a spoonful of chopped mushroom in the base of each ham cup and sprinkle half a tablespoon of cheese on top of the mushrooms.

Season the beaten egg with salt and pepper and divide it evenly among the cups.

Place the muffin cups in the hot oven and cook for 15 – 20 minutes until the egg is set. Do not overcook as the mixture will go rubbery.

Remove from the oven and serve.

Looking for something easy, different and tasty all at the same time? Add whatever you fancy to the cups – chopped green onion, herbs, spices such as powdered paprika and cayenne or even some chopped crispy bacon.

INGREDIENTS

6 **large thin slices cured ham**

6 **small mushrooms**, finely chopped

3 tbsp. **mozzarella cheese**, shredded

6 **large fresh eggs**, beaten

Salt and pepper to season

NUTRITONAL FACTS
per cup

Calories 151, Fat 8.8g, Carbohydrate 1.2g, Dietary Fiber 0.1g, Net Carbs 1.1g, Protein 16.2g

EGGS BENEDICT

You too can enjoy this classy breakfast in your own home.
No need to visit a 5 star restaurant for this enjoyable start to the day.

Serves 4

DIRECTIONS

Place the egg yolks, 3 tablespoons of lemon juice and the salt in a blender to make the Hollandaise sauce.

Set the blender on high and **slowly** add the warm, melted butter – **this is important** – do not add all of the butter at once otherwise the sauce will separate.

When you have finished blending it should be a glossy thick sauce.

Remove the sauce from the blender and place in a glass bowl.

Heat some water in a deep skillet and poach the 4 whole eggs until the whites are cooked but the yolks are still runny.

Serve on individual plates: thick slices of fried bacon topped by a poached egg and then a spoonful or two of sauce.

Garnish with pepper, paprika and fresh parsley.

INGREDIENTS

4 whole **large fresh eggs**

4 **egg yolks**

8 **slices bacon**, fried

6 ounces (170g) **butter**, melted and kept warm

3 tbsp. **lemon juice**, freshly squeezed

½ tsp. **salt**

Freshly cracked **black pepper**

Powdered paprika to garnish

4 sprigs **fresh parsley** to garnish

NUTRITONAL FACTS
per serve

Calories 549, Fat 46.8g, Carbohydrate 3.7g, Dietary Fiber 0.8g, Net Carbs 2.9g, Protein 27.5g

BREAKY BISCUITS

Makes 6

DIRECTIONS

Pre-heat the oven to 350°F (177°C).

Grease a large cookie sheet or cover it with non-stick parchment paper.

In a large bowl mix together the coconut flour, ground flaxseed, salt and baking powder.

Pour in the melted butter and rub the ingredients together with your hands to form breadcrumbs.

Add the eggs to the mixture and mix well together.

Place spoonfuls onto the baking sheet, well apart.

The mixture will be quite loose.

Place in the oven and bake for 15 – 20 minutes until brown.

Leave to cool on the cookie sheet for about 5 minutes before transferring to a wire rack to cool completely.

A handy recipe for a breakfast biscuit which you could top with melted cheese, a slice of bacon or some chopped green onion mixed into cream cheese.
They are also good just as they are, spread with some delectable farm butter.

NUTRITONAL FACTS
per biscuit

Calories 215, Fat 15.9g, Carbohydrate 10.6g, Dietary Fiber 7.6g, Net Carbs 3.0g, Protein 11.1g

INGREDIENTS

1½ ounces (43g) **coconut flour**

3½ ounces (99g) **flaxseed meal**

½ tsp. **salt**

3 tsp. **baking powder**

2 tbsp. **butter**, melted

6 **large fresh eggs**, beaten

AVOCADO EGGS

Tasty tropical flavors for breakfast give the morning a sunny start even on the chilliest winter's day.

INGREDIENTS

12 **large fresh eggs**

3 tbsp. **heavy cream**

2 tbsp. **butter**

½ **small onion**, finely chopped

1 clove **garlic**, finely chopped

3 **medium ripe tomatoes**, skinned, seeded and chopped

1 **jalapeno chili**, finely chopped (seeded for a milder flavor)

1½ tbsp. **fresh cilantro**, finely chopped

1 tbsp. **fresh lime juice**

1 cup (113g) **cheddar cheese**, shredded

1 **large avocado**, skinned and chopped

6 tbsp. **sour cream**

Salt and pepper to taste

Serves 6

DIRECTIONS

The evening before, mix together the onion, garlic, tomatoes, chili, cilantro and lime juice in a ceramic bowl.

Cover and refrigerate overnight for the flavors to blend.

In the morning: Remove the salsa mix from the refrigerator and allow it to reach room temperature.

Break the eggs and beat well together with the cream and season to taste.

In a large skillet, heat the butter until melted and add the eggs.

Scramble the eggs as desired.

Portion the eggs out onto individual serve plates and top with the pre-made salsa, avocado, cheese and the sour cream.

NUTRITONAL FACTS
per serve

Calories 392, Fat 32.1g, Carbohydrate 8.7g, Dietary Fiber 3.3g, Net Carbs 5.4g, Protein 19.3g

TURKEY EGGS

Serves 6

DIRECTIONS

Heat the oil in a large non – stick skillet over a medium high heat.

Add the onion and stir fry for a few minutes until it softens.

Add the ground turkey and stir fry with the onion until brown.

Break up any large pieces of turkey as you fry it.

Drain half of the oil from the skillet.

Add the cream cheese and spinach to the turkey and onion mixture and mix it in well.

Season the beaten eggs with salt and pepper and whisk in the cold water.

Pour the eggs over the turkey and cream cheese mixture.

Cook the eggs gently. Every now and then carefully lift the sides of the omelet to allow some of the uncooked egg to go to the bottom of the skillet.

The egg should still be soft but cooked in the middle.

If you like your omelet a little more cooked put it under a hot griddle to finish cooking the center and brown the top.

When cooked slide the omelet onto a serve dish, fold in half if you want to and serve. Don't worry if it cracks!

NUTRITONAL FACTS
per serve

Calories 443, Fat 32.7g, Carbohydrate 3.4g, Dietary Fiber 0.4g, Net Carbs 3.0g, Protein 34.8g

This is a ground turkey and cheese omelet style dish which can be flavored as you wish with fresh herbs for freshness, some chili for a bit heat or a topping of grated cheddar for an extra cheesy zing.

INGREDIENTS

1½ pounds (681g) **ground turkey meat**

1 **medium onion**, very finely chopped

2 tbsp. **olive oil**

1 cup (232g) **cream cheese**

½ cup (90g) **cooked spinach**, drained and chopped

9 **large fresh eggs**, beaten

2½ tbsp. **cold water**

Salt and pepper to taste

KETO B.L.T.

Using cheese crisps as a bun? What is this delicious, dark magic?! Scrumptious, quick and so simple! Those bread eaters don't know what they are missing.

INGREDIENTS

1 cup (113g) **mozzarella cheese**, grated

4 **slices bacon**, cooked until crispy

2 **small tomatoes**, thinly sliced

¼ cup (59ml) **creamy mayonnaise**

4 **large butter lettuce leaves**

Salt and pepper to season

Watercress to garnish

Serves 4

DIRECTIONS

Preheat the oven to 375°F (191°C).

Prepare a baking sheet by lining it with non-stick parchment.

Divide the cheese into 8 serves and place these on the baking sheet, leaving a space between them.

Place in the hot oven until they have spread a little, melted and golden brown.

Remove from the oven and cool a little before transferring to a cooking rack to cool and crisp completely.

Top a mozzarella crisp with a little mayonnaise, a slice of bacon, a couple of slices of tomato, and some lettuce.

Season to taste.

Complete with another mozzarella crisp.

Serve.

NUTRITONAL FACTS
per serve

Calories 284, Fat 23.8g, Carbohydrate 2.9g, Dietary Fiber 0.6g, Net Carbs 2.3g, Protein 14.5g

BACON & SAUSAGE PIE

A gratifying recipe, a little reminiscent of a British Toad in the Hole, but with a Keto twist. If you have room for a couple more low GI carbs, serve this with a slice or two of grilled tomato.

DIRECTIONS

Skin the sausages and place the meat in a bowl.

Add the minced bacon and mix well together.

With damp hands form the sausage mixture into small balls the size of a walnut.

Heat the olive oil in a large skillet over a medium high heat.

Fry the sausage balls in the oil until nicely browned.

Remove from the heat and drain of paper towel.

Pre heat the oven to 350°F (177°C).

Prepare a medium sized roasting pan by greasing it lightly with butter.

In a large bowl, mix together the coconut flour, baking soda, cayenne, thyme and some seasoning.

In a separate bowl mix together the coconut oil, coconut milk, lemon juice and eggs. Beat well together.

Add the liquid mixture to the dry ingredients.

Stir in half of the cheese.

Pour into the prepared roasting pan.

Place the sausage balls evenly into the batter.

Sprinkle with the remaining cheese.

Bake in the hot oven for 30 – 40 minutes until brown.

Remove from the oven and serve piping hot.

INGREDIENTS

6 **chicken sausages**

6 **rashers bacon**, minced

1½ cups (170g) **Cheddar cheese**, shredded

¾ cup (84g) **coconut flour**

¾ cup (178ml) **coconut oil**

⅓ cup (78ml) **coconut milk**

7 **large fresh eggs**

1 **lemon**, juiced

2 tsp. **fresh thyme**, finely chopped

½ tsp. **powdered cayenne pepper**

1 tsp. **baking soda**

2 tbsp. **olive oil**

Butter for greasing

Salt and pepper to season

NUTRITONAL FACTS
per serve

Calories 548, Fat 46.8g, Carbohydrate 10.0g, Dietary Fiber 4.4g, Net Carbs 5.6g, Protein 22.4g

WHICH CAME FIRST? SCOTCH EGGS

The proverbial chicken and the egg come together in this dish for a delicious combination.

INGREDIENTS

6 large eggs

2 large fresh eggs, beaten

20 ounces (567g) **fresh chicken breast**, finely ground

Salt and pepper to taste

1½ cups (105g) **pork skins**, crisped and crushed

Oil for deep frying

Makes 6

DIRECTIONS

Hard boil the 6 large eggs.

Cool and peel. Dry thoroughly.

Mix the beaten egg into the chicken meat and season well with salt and pepper.

Divide the chicken into 6 portions.

Form each piece into a circle large enough to wrap around the eggs.

Carefully wrap each egg making sure that there are no parts of the eggs left uncovered.

Place in the fridge for about an hour to 'set'.

Roll the eggs in the crushed pork skin.

Heat the oil until lightly smoking.

Carefully drop the eggs into it and fry gently on all sides until golden brown.

Remove from the oil and drain on paper towel.

Cool before cutting in half and serving.

NUTRITONAL FACTS
per scotch egg

Calories 319, Fat 18.4g, Carbohydrate 0.5g, Dietary Fiber 0g, Net Carbs 0.5g, Protein 36.5g

CREAM CHEESE & HERB OMELET

Serves 4

A deliciously simple, and oh-so-creamy omelet to start your day. Chives are a great herb option as they go so well with the cream cheese.

DIRECTIONS

Pre-heat a griddle to high.

Melt the butter in a large skillet over a medium high heat.

Break the eggs into a large bowl and add the water, herbs and seasoning.

Whisk well together until fluffy.

Pour into the hot skillet.

Using a spatula, carefully lift the edges of the omelet as it cooks to allow the raw egg to run underneath onto the base of the skillet.

When the omelet is nearly set place the skillet under the hot grill. The top of the omelet should puff up and brown.

Remove from the griddle and spoon the cream cheese on one side. Add the bacon halves.

Carefully fold the omelet over and cut into 4 serves to serve.

If preferred the omelet may be cooked in 4 batches, each one a single serve.

INGREDIENTS

8 **large fresh eggs**

2 tbsp. **butter**

3 tbsp. **fresh herbs**, finely chopped

4 tbsp. **cold water**

5 ounces (142g) **cream cheese**

Salt and pepper to season

8 **slices bacon**, crisped and each slice cut in half

NUTRITONAL FACTS
per serve

Calories 494, Fat 41.1g, Carbohydrate 2.3g, Dietary Fiber 0.0g, Net Carbs 2.3g, Protein 29.1g

BLUEBERRY PANCAKES

At around 4 net carbs each, this sweet pancake recipe will quickly become one of your favorites. Feel free to change the berries if you want to get creative, or halve the berries to go a little stricter on the carb intake.

Makes 8

DIRECTIONS

Sieve the flours, baking powder and cinnamon together in a large bowl.

Beat together the eggs, coconut milk, water, stevia drops and almond milk.

Add the egg mixture slowly to the flour, beating well so that no lumps are formed.

Heat a little butter in a large skillet and drop tablespoons of batter onto it when hot.

Put a few blueberries into the batter before it sets.

Allow to set on the base before flipping over and cooking the top for a few moments.

Remove from the skillet and keep warm in a clean tea towel while cooking the rest.

Serve with sugar free syrup and enjoy.

INGREDIENTS

¾ cup (178ml) **coconut milk**

½ cup (119ml) **water**

¼ cup (59ml) **almond milk**

1½ tsp. **baking powder**

½ cup (56g) **coconut flour**

¼ cup (24g) **almond flour**

1 tsp. **cinnamon**

3 drops **liquid stevia extract** (adjust to taste)

6 **eggs**

½ cup (74g) **fresh blueberries**

Butter for cooking

Sugar free syrup to serve

NUTRITONAL FACTS
per pancake

Calories 212, Fat 17.1g, Carbohydrate 8.5g, Dietary Fiber 3.9g, Net Carbs 4.6g, Protein 6.0g

FISH CAKES

Serves 8

DIRECTIONS

In a large bowl, gently fork together the white fish and the tuna.

Add the green onions and chopped parsley.

Add all of the spices, the medium eggs, mayonnaise and the chili sauce.

Mix gently together and season with salt and pepper.

Form the fish mixture into 8 balls and press each one down to form a 'cake'.

Place each of these very carefully onto a baking sheet lined with cling film.

Refrigerate for 1 hour.

Remove the cakes from the fridge and coat each one carefully in the remaining beaten egg followed by ground coconut.

Refrigerate again for 1 hour.

When you are ready to cook the fish cakes, heat some oil in a large skillet over a medium high heat.

Fry the cakes carefully until golden brown on both sides and heated through. This will take about 4 minutes on each side.

Remove the cakes from the oil and drain on kitchen towel.

Serve as desired.

NUTRITONAL FACTS
per serve

Calories 248, Fat 17.2g, Carbohydrate 2.0g, Dietary Fiber 0.9g, Net Carbs 1.1g, Protein 20.9g

Fish cakes for breakfast are an old favorite especially with kids. Serve with some low carb. tomato sauce or a spicy guacamole.
Refrigerate any extras you may have for the next day or freeze.

INGREDIENTS

10 ounces (284g) **canned tuna chunks**, drained and flaked

10 ounces (284g) cooked **firm white fish**, boned and flaked

⅓ cup (78ml) **mayonnaise**

2½ tbsp. **fresh parsley**, finely chopped

6 **green onions**, finely chopped

Pinch **celery salt**

Pinch **powdered paprika**

¼ tsp. **cayenne pepper**

½ tsp. **chili sauce**

2 **medium fresh eggs**, beaten

2 **large fresh eggs**, beaten

⅔ cup (74g) **unsweetened coconut**, ground finely

Salt and pepper to season

Olive oil for frying

INTREPID COFFEE

**Just the way to start any day – bold, fearless and courageous.
Enjoy this new twist on a modern favorite.**

Serves 2

DIRECTIONS

Pour the coffee into 2 mugs.

Stir in half of the coconut oil, sweetener and salt into each mug.

Stir thoroughly.

Add 1 tablespoon of cream into each cup and stir.

Whip the remaining cream until soft peaks.

Top each coffee with a dollop of whipped cream.

Sprinkle with a little cocoa powder.

Yum, enjoy!

INGREDIENTS

2 cups freshly brewed **coffee**

4 tbsp. **heavy cream**

1 tbsp. **coconut oil**

Sweetener (**stevia drops or erythritol powder**) to taste

2 pinches **sea salt**

Cocoa powder to sprinkle

NUTRITONAL FACTS
per serve

Calories 223, Fat 24.8g, Carbohydrate 0.8g, Dietary Fiber 0g, Net Carbs 0.8g, Protein 0.9g

28

OOPSIE FRENCH TOASTIES

Serves 3

The popular Oopsie rolls take on a different guise as French toast and are great served with sugar free syrup or just some yummy farm butter. Ultra nice with bacon, sausages or some shredded cheese sprinkled on top.

DIRECTIONS

Pre-heat oven to 300°F (149°C).

Cover a baking sheet with parchment paper.

Combine the egg yolks, sugar substitute, salt and cream cheese in a bowl. Beat well together – use a mixer if you have one.

Whisk together the egg whites and the cream of tartar until soft peaks.

Fold the whites carefully into the yolk mixture with a metal spoon. **Do not beat.**

Spoon the mixture onto the prepared baking sheet. Flatten each roll a little with the back of a spoon.

Bake for about 25 - 30 minutes until cooked through but still soft.

Remove from the oven and cool on a wire rack.

Beat together the egg, coconut cream, vanilla, cinnamon and a pinch of salt in a large shallow bowl.

Melt the butter in a large non-stick skillet over a medium high heat.

Dip the oopsie rolls in the egg mixture, one at a time and fry on one side until golden brown.

Flip over and cook on the other side.

Serve hot topped with sugar free syrup or butter.

INGREDIENTS

Oopsie rolls:

3 **large fresh eggs**, separated

2 tsp. **powdered sugar substitute**

1 pinch **salt**

1 pinch **cream of tartar**

3 ounces (85g) **plain cream cheese**

Sugar free syrup

Toastie Mix:

3 **large fresh eggs**

¼ cup (59ml) **coconut cream**

1 tsp. **vanilla extract**

1 tsp. **powdered cinnamon**

4 ounces (113g) **butter**

Pinch of **salt**

NUTRITONAL FACTS
per serve

Calories 579, Fat 55.3g, Carbohydrate 4.6g, Dietary Fiber 0.6g, Net Carbs 4.0g, Protein 15.6g

LUNCH

EGGPLANT FRITTATA

An easy dish to make for a quick luncheon shared with family or friends. For a smaller frittata halve the ingredients and cook it in a smaller skillet. This is especially good with a green salad to add a little crunch.

INGREDIENTS

8 **large fresh eggs**

3 **shallots**, finely chopped

1 **small onion**, finely chopped

3 cloves **garlic**, finely chopped

1¼ pounds (568g), peeled weight, **eggplant**, diced

3 ounces (85g) **mature Cheddar cheese**, shredded

1 tbsp. **fresh parsley**, finely chopped

1 tsp. **fresh thyme**, finely chopped

Salt and pepper to season

Butter for frying

Serves 6

DIRECTIONS

In a large skillet with a lid, heat the butter until melted.

Carefully sauté the shallot and onion until translucent – be careful not to burn the butter.

Add the egg plant and cook everything together for a few minutes until the eggplant is soft.

In a medium sized bowl whisk the eggs together with the parsley and thyme.

Stir in the shredded cheese.

Pour over the eggplant, mix together gently.

Cover the pancake with the skillet lid and continue to cook over a medium-low heat until the egg mixture is set.

Remove from the heat when ready and serve.

NUTRITONAL FACTS
per serve

Calories 195, Fat 13.5g, Carbohydrate 6.8g, Dietary Fiber 3.3g, Net Carbs 3.5g, Protein 13.0g

CRUNCHY COBB SALAD

Serves 4

An amazing dish to which you can add whatever you fancy such as cooked chicken or turkey slices. Use a milder blue cheese if you prefer for the dressing - Dolce bleu is a good choice.

DIRECTIONS

In a small bowl mix together the mayonnaise, milk, cream, lemon juice and seasoning to taste.

Set aside in a serve jug in the fridge.

In 4 individual serve dishes layer the rest of the salad ingredients; lettuce, ham, egg, bell pepper, cucumber, bacon, Gorgonzola and avocado.

Top with watercress.

Serve the salad together with the cream dressing.

INGREDIENTS

½ cup (119ml) **mayonnaise**

¼ cup (59ml) **unsweetened almond milk**

½ cup (118ml) **heavy cream**

½ tsp. **lemon juice**

¼ head **iceberg lettuce**, washed and torn

1 **small bunch watercress**, washed

2 **slices ham**, chopped

2 **slices bacon**, cooked and chopped

1 **large egg**, hard boiled and coarsely chopped

14 inch (36cm) **cucumber**, peeled, seeded and chopped

1 **small red bell pepper**, seeded and chopped

⅓ cup (45g) **Gorgonzola cheese**, crumbled

1 **ripe avocado**, peeled and chopped

Salt and pepper to season

NUTRITONAL FACTS
per serve

Calories 524, Fat 50.1g, Carbohydrate 11.2g, Dietary Fiber 5.0g, Net Carbs 6.2g, Protein 11.3g

PEPPERONI & SUNDRIED TOMATO PIZZA

I love the tantalizing taste of a good pepperoni pizza and nobody can take that away from me (just try). This enticing and savory Keto version has saved my sanity on more than one occasion!

INGREDIENTS

Base:

1 cup (113g) **mozzarella cheese**, shredded

1 cup (113g) **strong Cheddar cheese**, shredded

2 tbsp. **cream cheese**

4 ounces (113g) **almond flour**

1 **extra-large fresh egg**

Topping:

3 ounces (85g) chopped **pepperoni**

¼ tsp. **dried oregano**

¼ cup (28g) **sundried tomatoes in olive oil**, chopped

¾ cup (99g) sliced **mozzarella cheese**

½ cup (21g) fresh **basil leaves**, torn

Makes 8 slices

DIRECTIONS

Pre-heat the oven to 425°F (218°C).

Prepare a cookie sheet by covering it with non-stick parchment paper.

Gently melt the shredded cheeses together in ceramic bowl in a microwave or over a pan of boiling water.

Cool a little before kneading in the almond flour, cream cheese and the egg.

When a smooth dough is formed spread it out thinly on the prepared cookie sheet.

You can use your hands for this or roll it between 2 sheets of parchment.

Place the cookie sheet in the hot oven and bake for 10 – 15 minutes until it begins to brown around the edges.

Remove from the oven and top with the pepperoni, sun dried tomatoes, sliced mozzarella and the oregano.

Place the pizza back in the oven to heat the topping trough and melt the cheese – about 5 minutes.

Remove from the oven and sprinkle on the torn basil leaves.

Slice and serve.

NUTRITONAL FACTS
per slice

Calories 290, Fat 23.3g, Carbohydrate 5.1g, Dietary Fiber 1.7g, Net Carbs 3.4g, Protein 16.6g

CHICKEN CRUNCH SALAD

Serves 6

Try this mouth-watering fresh lunch that's so simple to put together. Easily reduce quantities to make less serves.

DIRECTIONS

In a large bowl, gently toss together the cooked chicken, celery, bell pepper and green onions.

Mix together the mayonnaise, sour cream and the dill pickle in a separate bowl.

Add the mayonnaise mix to the chicken and vegetables and toss carefully together. Season to taste.

Spoon the mixture onto lettuce leaves to serve.

Decorate with the egg quarters and sprinkle with the pecan nuts.

INGREDIENTS

4 cooked **chicken breasts**, skinned and diced

2 sticks **celery**, washed and finely sliced

1 **small yellow bell pepper**, seeded and sliced into rings

3 **green onions**, sliced

3 **dill pickles**, finely chopped

¾ cup (178ml) **mayonnaise**

2 tbsp. **sour cream**

3 **large fresh eggs**, boiled, peeled and quartered

½ cup (55g) chopped **pecan nuts**

Salt and pepper to season

Lettuce leaves to serve

NUTRITONAL FACTS
per serve

Calories 509, Fat 36.2g, Carbohydrate 4.4g, Dietary Fiber 2.2g, Net Carbs 2.2g, Protein 40.1g

CUCUMBER, HAM & FETA SALAD

This is an exquisite light salad for those hot summer days when you don't really feel like cooking or spending time in the kitchen. The cucumber adds a lovely succulent crunch.

INGREDIENTS

2 **large cucumbers**

6 ounces (170g) **feta cheese**, crumbled

8 ounces (227g) **cooked ham**, in one slice, cubed

2 tbsp. **fresh dill**, chopped

2 **large green onions**, finely sliced

Salt and pepper to season

Drizzle of **extra virgin olive oil**

Walnuts to garnish

Serves 4

DIRECTIONS

Slice the cucumbers lengthwise into quarters and remove the seeds.

Slice the cucumber quarters into ¼ inch (0.6cm) slices.

Place the slices into a large salad bowl.

Add the ham and the feta cheese to the cucumber.

Sprinkle over the green onion and the dill.

Season to taste and drizzle over a little olive oil.

Garnish with whole or chopped walnuts.

NUTRITONAL FACTS
per serve

Calories 256, Fat 16.0g, Carbohydrate 8.4g, Dietary Fiber 2.3g, Net Carbs 6.1g, Protein 20.3g

SUMMERY THAI SEAFOOD SALAD

Serves 3

The fresher the seafood the better. Perfect for a lazy, hazy summer day and replete with Thai overtones to transport you on an adventure with every bite. This salad will fit well amongst your repertoire of Keto foodie creations.

DIRECTIONS

Heat the wine and water a large saucepan with a lid over a medium high.

When boiling add the seafood and the parsley.

Cover and simmer for 4 minutes.

Remove from the heat and take out the seafood.

Leave to cool.

Meanwhile mix together, in a blender, lime juice, olive oil, sesame oil, soy sauce, green ginger, garlic, chili and liquid sweetener.

Season to taste and pour into a jug to serve.

When ready to serve arrange the seafood on separate plates.

Top with the green onion, tomato and red pepper.

Divide the seafood among the plates.

Serve with the Thai dressing.

Add parsley or cilantro to taste.

INGREDIENTS

2 pounds (907g) **mixed fresh seafood**; i.e. shrimp, calamari, white meat fish or lobster, all shelled and cleaned

⅓ cup (78ml) **white wine**

1 cup (237ml) **water**

2 tbsp. **chopped parsley**

½ **red pepper**, seeded and sliced

3 **green onions**, sliced

1 **large tomato**, seeded

2 tbsp. **fresh lime juice**

3 tbsp. **olive oil**

½ tbsp. **sesame oil**

½ tbsp. **soy sauce**

1 tsp. **green ginger**, finely grated

1 clove **garlic**, finely grated

1 **small fresh chili**, seeded and finely chopped

3 drops **liquid stevia extract** (adjust to taste)

Flat leafed parsley or cilantro to serve

Salt and pepper to season

NUTRITONAL FACTS
per serve

Calories 186, Fat 9.6g, Carbohydrate 4.3g, Dietary Fiber 0.8g, Net Carbs 3.5g, Protein 18.0g

HAM & CAULIFLOWER CHEESE

Cauliflower cheese is one of those dishes that get handed down through the family from one generation to the next. Every family has their favorite version, this one with ham, Cheddar and Gruyere for a unique tang.

INGREDIENTS

1½ pounds (681g) **cauliflower**, broken into bite sized florets

8 ounces (227g) **ham**, in a single slice and chopped

1½ cups (356ml) **plain Greek yogurt**

4 ounces (113g) **Cheddar cheese**, shredded

6 ounces (170g) **Gruyere cheese**, shredded

3 **green onions**, finely sliced

2 tsp. **readymade English mustard**

1 tsp. **powdered paprika**

Butter to grease

Salt and pepper to season

Serves 4

DIRECTIONS

Heat some water in a large sauce pan and when it is boiling add the cauliflower.

Boil for 8 – 10 minutes until al dente. Drain very well in a colander.

Pre-heat the oven to 375°F (191°C).

Butter a medium sized, deep casserole dish.

Place the well-drained cauliflower in the dish and sprinkle over the chopped ham and the green onions.

Season with salt and pepper.

In a separate bowl mix together the yogurt, mustard, Cheddar cheese, paprika and half of the Gruyere cheese.

Pour this over the cauliflower.

Sprinkle the top with the rest of the Gruyere and place uncovered in the hot oven.

Bake for 30 – 35 minutes until hot, bubbly and brown on top.

Remove from the oven and let the dish stand for 5 minutes before serve.

NUTRITONAL FACTS
per serve

Calories 558, Fat 36.8g, Carbohydrate 14.6g, Dietary Fiber 4.7g, Net Carbs 9.9g, Protein 43.3g

CHICKEN & VEGETABLE STRATA

Serves 4

An Italian style omelet, and a great way to use chicken sausages. Swap in other types of sausage for variety and use herbs instead of the sundried tomatoes if you wish.

DIRECTIONS

Heat the oil in a large skillet over a medium high heat.

Fry the sausages until golden brown on all sides.

Remove from the skillet, drain on kitchen towel and leave to cool.

Put the broccoli in the same skillet and sauté for a few minutes until brown.

Cool.

Pre-heat the oven to 350°F (177°C).

Prepare a 10 inch (25cm) oven proof pan by brushing it with a little oil.

When the sausages are cool, dice them and place in the prepared pan.

Sprinkle the broccoli over the sausage.

Sprinkle the chopped sun dried tomatoes over the sausage and broccoli.

Add seasoning to the beaten eggs.

Gently pour the egg over the sausage mixture.

Place in the oven and bake for 30 – 35 minutes until the egg is set and the frittata is nicely browned on the top.

Remove from the oven and cool a little before slicing and serve with the torn baby spinach on the side.

INGREDIENTS

8 **chicken sausages**

8 **large fresh eggs**, beaten

1 cup (91g) **broccoli**, chopped

1 cup (30g) **baby spinach**, torn

2 tbsp. **sundried tomatoes in olive oil**, chopped

1 tbsp. **olive oil**

Salt and pepper to season

Oil for brushing

NUTRITONAL FACTS
per serve

Calories 371, Fat 26.2g, Carbohydrate 8.7g, Dietary Fiber 1.4g, Net Carbs 7.3g, Protein 24.0g

CHUNKY FARMHOUSE PÂTÉ

French inspired and wonderful for lunch or any time of the day. It will keep for a few days in the fridge for you to enjoy – that is of course if there is any left. Serve with a green salad and some sliced hard boiled eggs.

INGREDIENTS

16 ounces (454g) **pork belly meat**, coarsely ground

8 ounces (227g) **chicken livers**, trimmed

¾ cup (178ml) **unsweetened almond milk**

1 **large onion**, finely chopped

3 tbsp. **chicken broth**

½ cup (56g) **flaxseed meal**

1 **large fresh egg**

1 **large lemon**, zest only

12 **slices bacon**

1 tbsp. **fresh thyme**, finely chopped

Salt and pepper to season

Serves 10

DIRECTIONS

Soak the liver in the milk for 30 minutes.

Pre-heat the oven to 375°F (191°C).

Remove the liver and pat dry.

Place in a processor and pulse until smooth.

Prepare a 2 pound (907g) loaf tin or dish by lining it with the bacon slices.

In a large bowl mix together all of the remaining ingredients and add the liver.

Be careful when seasoning with salt as the bacon will provide salt as the pâté cooks.

Carefully spoon the mixture into the bacon lined dish, folding over any bacon slices that may stick up above the filling.

Cover the dish with foil and place it in a roasting pan filled with water to a depth of 2 inches (5cm).

Place the roasting pan in the pre-heated oven and cook for 1½ - 1¾ hours.

The juices should run clear when a knife is inserted into the pâté.

Remove from the oven when done and take the dish out of the roasting pan.

Do not pour off the juices around the pâté.

Leave to cool before slicing.

A weight may be placed atop the pâté to compress it for a few hours before slicing, and serving.

NUTRITONAL FACTS
per serve

Calories 522, Fat 46.3g, Carbohydrate 4.1g, Dietary Fiber 2.0g, Net Carbs 2.1g, Protein 22.4g

SALMON & AVOCADO BOATS

Makes 4 Boats

Avocado halves filled with a yummy mixture of salmon and tangy mayonnaise.
These don't keep so make just enough for your needs.
Try cayenne pepper instead of paprika if you would like to add a little heat.

DIRECTIONS

Cut each avocado in half lengthwise. Remove the pip.

Scoop out some of the flesh from each avocado with a small spoon, leaving a wall of about ¾ inch (2cm).

Place the avocado flesh in a small bowl.

Finely chop the salmon.

Mix the salmon into the avocado in the bowl.

Add the lemon juice, mayonnaise and cream cheese.

Mix in the chopped green onions and seasoning to taste.

Divide the salmon mixture evenly among the avocado halves.

Sprinkle with powdered paprika.

INGREDIENTS

2 **ripe but firm avocados**

7 ounces (198g) **smoked salmon pieces**

3 tbsp. **mayonnaise**

3 tbsp. **cream cheese**

2 **green onions**, finely chopped

2 tbsp. **freshly squeezed lemon juice**

½ tsp. **powdered paprika**

Salt and pepper to season

NUTRITONAL FACTS
per boat

Calories 371, Fat 33.1g, Carbohydrate 9.6g, Dietary Fiber 7.0g, Net Carbs 2.6g, Protein 11.8g

AVOCADO & TOMATO CHEESE SALAD

A deliciously easy salad to add a sparkle to your day. So quick to prepare.

Serves 4

INGREDIENTS

4 **medium avocados**, peeled and sliced

6 **small ripe tomatoes**, skinned and chopped

1 **small red onion**, finely chopped

1 cup (42g) **fresh basil leaves**, torn

6 ounces (170g) **fresh mozzarella cheese,** broken into bite sized pieces

¼ cup (59ml) **extra virgin olive oil**

2 tsp. **white wine vinegar**

Salt and pepper to taste

DIRECTIONS

Toss the avocado, tomatoes and onion together lightly.

Sprinkle with the oil and vinegar and lightly toss again.

Cover and refrigerate for 30 minutes for the flavors to mingle.

Remove from the refrigerator and add the cheese.

Spoon carefully into serve bowls.

Top with the torn basil leaves.

NUTRITONAL FACTS
per serve

Calories 554, Fat 49.7g, Carbohydrate 21.5g, Dietary Fiber 12.2g, Net Carbs 9.3g, Protein 11.9g

SALMON NORI ROLLS

Makes 12

Sushi without rice is the perfect Keto twist for this Asian inspired lunch.

DIRECTIONS

Lay out the nori sheets individually with the shiny side down on a sushi mat if you have one. If not, plastic wrap works well!

Divide the salmon slices in two and lay them over the bottom half of each nori sheet.

Place the avocado and cucumber slices on top of the salmon about 1 inch (2.5cm) from the edge.

Beat the wasabi paste into the cream cheese.

Spoon the cream cheese along the avocado and cucumber as evenly as you can.

Start rolling from the salmon end – like a Swiss roll.

Use the sushi mat or plastic wrap to help you. Press firmly as you go so that the nori sticks together. Use a damp finger if necessary to help 'stick' the edges together.

With a very sharp knife cut each roll into 6 even sized pieces.

Serve with the pickled ginger slices and soy sauce for dipping.

INGREDIENTS

2 **sheets nori** (dried seaweed)

6 ounces (170g) **sliced smoked salmon**

½ **small avocado**, peeled and thinly sliced

1 x **cucumber**, sliced into 2 inch (5cm) pieces, seeded and julienned

4 ounces (113g) **cream cheese**

1 tsp. **wasabi paste** (to taste)

Pickled ginger and soy sauce to serve

NUTRITONAL FACTS
per roll

Calories 76, Fat 5.7g, Carbohydrate 2.7g, Dietary Fiber 0.9g, Net Carbs 1.8g, Protein 4.1g

ASIAN CHICKEN WRAPS & SATAY SAUCE

These chicken wraps use lettuce leaves to hold the scrumptious filling. Serve with spoonfuls of macadamia satay sauce drizzled on the top.

Serves 6

INGREDIENTS

12 outside leaves of a **butter lettuce**

3 cups (420g) **fresh chicken breast**, diced

1 **shallot**, finely chopped

3 cloves **garlic**, finely chopped

2 tsp. **green ginger**, grated

1 tbsp. **olive oil**

2 tsp. **sesame oil**

5 drops **liquid stevia extract** (adjust to taste)

1 **lime**, zest and juice

1 tbsp. **tomato paste**

1 **small red chili**, diced

Salt and pepper to taste

3 **green onions**, chopped

½ **small carrot**, peeled and shredded

Sauce:

1 **shallot**, peeled and chopped

1 clove **garlic**, finely minced

½ tsp. **fresh chili**, minced

Pinch **powdered ginger**

1 tsp. **mild and spicy curry powder**

¾ cup (178ml) **coconut cream**

1 tsp. **sesame oil**

3 drops **liquid stevia extract** (adjust to taste)

1/3 cup (38g) **toasted macadamia nuts**, finely chopped

1 tbsp. **peanut oil**

Salt and pepper to season

DIRECTIONS

Make the sauce first to allow the flavors to develop.

Heat the peanut oil in a small skillet over a medium high heat and stir-fry the shallot, garlic and chili for a couple of minutes until the shallot is tender.

Add all of the other sauce ingredients and combine well.

Season, and thin with a little water if required.

Pour the sauce into a small jug, set aside and keep warm.

Heat the olive oil in a large skillet and stir fry the chicken pieces until nearly cooked through.

Add the chopped shallot, garlic and ginger.

Stir fry for a minute longer.

Add the rest of the ingredients except the green onion, carrot and lettuce and cook together for a few minutes for the flavors to develop.

Remove from the skillet and set aside to cool.

Serve in the lettuce leaves sprinkled with some green onion and a little shredded carrot.

Serve the sauce separately and drizzle as required.

NUTRITONAL FACTS
per serve

Calories 327, Fat 22.5g, Carbohydrate 7.7g, Dietary Fiber 2.6g, Net Carbs 5.1g, Protein 26.2g

CREAM CHEESE & AVOCADO SHAKE

Makes 4

In a hurry? No problem.
Fix this simple nutritious shake to get you going for the day.

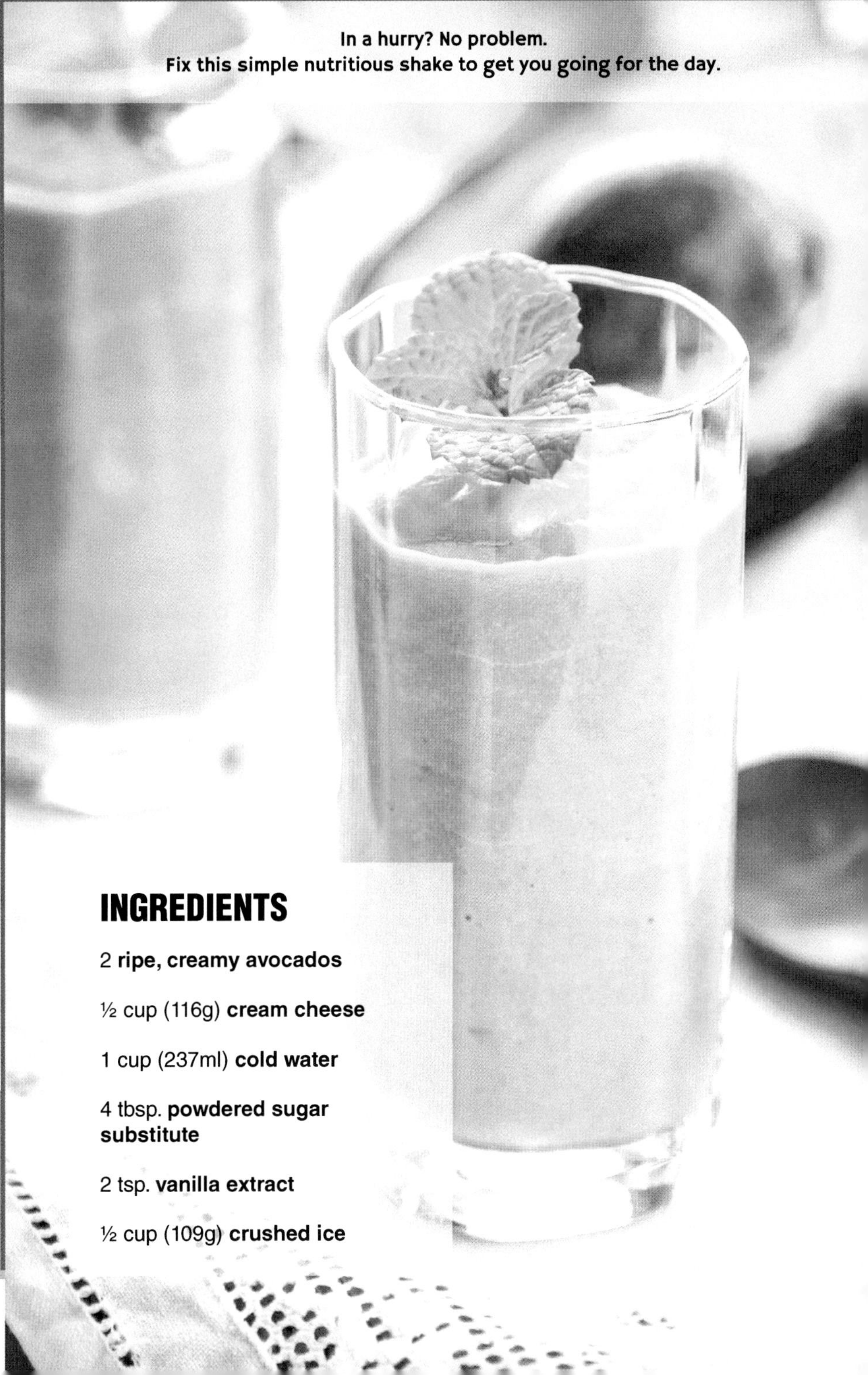

DIRECTIONS

Cut the avocados in half, remove the pip and scoop out the flesh into a blender.

Add the cream cheese, water, sugar substitute, vanilla and the crushed ice.

Pulse at first and then blend until smooth.

Pour into 2 glasses.

INGREDIENTS

2 **ripe, creamy avocados**

½ cup (116g) **cream cheese**

1 cup (237ml) **cold water**

4 tbsp. **powdered sugar substitute**

2 tsp. **vanilla extract**

½ cup (109g) **crushed ice**

NUTRITONAL FACTS

per glass

Calories 315, Fat 29.7g, Carbohydrate 10.4g, Dietary Fiber 6.7g, Net Carbs 3.7g, Protein 4.4g

STARTERS

PORK BELLY SLICES

Make use of pork belly slices to create this tasty meat dish. Cook as per this recipe in the oven, or socially over a barbeque if the day feels right! Garnish with crisp fresh watercress and thinly sliced cucumber.

Serves 8

INGREDIENTS

2 pounds (908g) **pork belly**, sliced into ¼ inch rashers

3 cloves **garlic**, very finely chopped

3 tbsp. **chili paste** (to taste)

1½ tbsp. grated **green ginger**

1 **large shallot**, well washed and finely chopped

3 tsp. **powdered sugar substitute**

2 tbsp. **sesame oil**

Salt and pepper to season

DIRECTIONS

Pre-heat the oven to 425°F (218°C).

In a small ceramic bowl, mix together the garlic, chili paste, grated ginger, sugar substitute, shallot and sesame oil.

Stir everything together well.

Brush this sauce onto the pork rashers and place them in a roasting tin.

Place the pork rashers into the hot oven and roast until crisp and golden brown, about 20 minutes.

Turn the rashers about half way through the cooking time.

Remove the rashers from the oven and drain them on some paper towel to remove any excess fat that may have come from the pork.

Serve warm.

NUTRITONAL FACTS
per serve

Calories 651, Fat 66.1g, Carbohydrate 3.3g, Dietary Fiber 0.1g, Net Carbs 3.2g, Protein 8.5g

PEPPERONI CHEESE EGGS

Serves 6

These tasty little morsels are a great starter to any meal. After these your taste buds will tingle in anticipation of what is still to come. Garnish with some arugula, watercress or salsa.

DIRECTIONS

Pre-heat the oven to 375°F (191°C).

Cut the squash in half, remove the seeds. Use a large serrated knife to do this as squash can be hard to cut.

Place the halves cut side down in a roasting tin and bake in the hot oven for 40 – 45 minutes until tender.

Remove squash from the oven and leave until cool.

Using a fork, scrape the flesh out of the shells and place in a large bowl.

You will need approximately 3 cups of 'spaghetti' for this recipe. (Store any leftover squash in the refrigerator for another meal).

Add the mozzarella, parsley, garlic, green onion and olive oil to the squash and mix well. Season to taste.

Butter 6 individual 8 ounce (227g) ramekins or oven proof dishes. Place them on a baking tin.

Divide the squash mixture evenly among the dishes.

Press the squash down a little and sprinkle the chopped pepperoni on top.

Crack the eggs, one at a time, into a cup and then carefully slide it onto the top of the pepperoni.

Season the egg with salt and pepper. Sprinkle with some Parmesan cheese.

Place in the hot oven and cook for 18 – 25 minutes.

Remove from the oven when the eggs are cooked.

Serve in the dishes, on clean individual plates.

NUTRITONAL FACTS
per serve

Calories 315, Fat 26.5g, Carbohydrate 6.7g, Dietary Fiber 0.1g, Net Carbs 6.6g, Protein 14.5g

INGREDIENTS

1 **medium spaghetti squash**

⅓ cup (38g) **mozzarella cheese**, shredded

¼ cup (15g) **fresh parsley**, finely chopped

1 clove **garlic**, finely chopped

1 **green onion**, finely chopped

¼ cup (59ml) **olive oil**

3 ounces (85g) **pepperoni**, finely diced

6 **large fresh eggs**

Salt and pepper to season

Butter for greasing

Parmesan cheese to sprinkle

CHINESE CHICKEN WINGS

Chicken wings are some of the tastiest and most enjoyable parts of a chicken and these sticky, saucy ones are no exception.
Remember to keep some extra paper napkins close by!

Serves 6

DIRECTIONS

In a large ceramic bowl, mix together all of the ingredients except the chicken wings and sesame seeds.

Lay out the chicken wings in a large flat dish and cover them with the soy sauce mixture.

Place in the fridge and marinate for 2 hours.

Just before you are ready to cook , pre-heat the oven to 350°F (177°C).

Transfer the chicken wings with their marinade into a large roasting tin, preferably in a single layer.

Place the wings in the oven and cook for 30 – 40 minutes until cooked and sticky.

Turn the wings half way through the cooking time to ensure an even coating of sauce.

Remove from the oven and serve sprinkled with sesame seeds.

INGREDIENTS

18 **chicken wings**, wing tips discarded

¾ cup (178ml) **light soy sauce**

¼ cup (59ml) **dark soy sauce**

2 tbsp. **granulated sugar substitute**

4 tbsp. **dry white wine**

3 cloves **garlic**, very finely chopped

1 tsp. **powdered ginger**

3 tbsp. **sesame oil**

Salt and pepper to season

Sesame seeds to sprinkle

NUTRITONAL FACTS
per serve

Calories 355, Fat 26.2g, Carbohydrate 4.7g, Dietary Fiber 0.6g, Net Carbs 4.1g, Protein 26.0g

SMOKED MACKEREL CRUNCH PARCELS

A cheesy mackerel pâté served wrapped in crisp iceberg lettuce leaves; ideal for a family snack or to serve for friends. The filled rolls do not keep so munch away and enjoy.

DIRECTIONS

Place all of the ingredients into a food processor except for the lettuce and pulse until well mixed and smooth.

Remove the mixture from the processor and place in a bowl.

Refrigerate for a couple of hours to allow the flavors to blend and develop.

When read to serve remove from the refrigerator and spoon equally into the middle of the lettuce leaves.

Carefully roll the lettuce leaves around the filling and serve on a plate.

INGREDIENTS

1 x 7 ounce (198g) can **smoked mackerel in oil**, drained and mashed

6 **fresh eggs**, hard boiled, peeled and mashed

2 tsp. **fresh parsley**, finely chopped

3 **large fresh eggs**, separated

12 ounces (340g) **cream cheese**

2 tsp. **fresh lemon juice**

3 **green onions**, finely sliced

6 **large crisp iceberg lettuce leaves**

Salt and pepper to taste

NUTRITONAL FACTS
per serve

Calories 406, Fat 35.0g, Carbohydrate 3.3g, Dietary Fiber 0.6g, Net Carbs 2.7g, Protein 20.3g

SPICY CHICKEN BALLS

Serve these on sticks to hand around to family or guests or thread on thin kebab skewers for a more substantial starter.
Serve warm or cold with sugar free chili or garlic chili sauce for extra zing.

Makes 24

DIRECTIONS

Heat 2 tbsp. oil in a large skillet and sauté the onions, bell pepper and the garlic.

Drain from the oil and leave in a small bowl to cool.

In a large bowl mix the chicken mince with the vegetables and all of the other ingredients except the oil.

Form into 1 inch (2.5cm) balls with damp hands.

Heat ½ inch (1.3cm) of oil in a clean skillet and fry the chicken balls, a few at a time, until nicely browned and cooked through.

When cooked remove from the oil and drain on paper towel.

Place each chicken ball on a toothpick or thread 3 or 4 onto a small skewer to serve.

INGREDIENTS

1½ pounds (681g) **chicken**, finely ground

1 **large onion**, very finely chopped

1 **small red bell pepper**, seeded and finely chopped

3 cloves **garlic**, crushed

2 tbsp. **soy sauce**

1 tbsp. **fresh lime juice**

½ tsp. **chili sauce**

½ tsp. **curry powder**

2 large fresh eggs

Salt and pepper to season

Olive oil for sautéing and frying

NUTRITONAL FACTS
per chicken ball

Calories 92, Fat 7.5g, Carbohydrate 1.1g, Dietary Fiber 0.3g, Net Carbs 0.8g, Protein 5.6g

SHRIMP SENSATION

Serves 6

DIRECTIONS

Season the shrimp with salt and pepper.

Heat the oil in a large skillet over a medium high heat.

Add the shrimp when the oil is hot and cook for a couple of minutes until they start to turn pink.

Add the garlic and chili flakes as well as the butter.

Continue to fry until the shrimp and garlic is cooked.

Remove the skillet from the heat and stir in the lemon juice and the parsley.

Serve whilst hot.

Garlic and shrimps are a marriage made in heaven. This recipe uses unpeeled shrimps to help seal in the flavor. The shrimps are easy to shell once cooked, but if you prefer you could use peeled. Warning, this is very garlicky!

INGREDIENTS

1½ pounds (681g) **raw shrimp**, cleaned (unpeeled)

2 tbsp. **peanut oil**

10 cloves **garlic**, finely chopped

½ tsp. **dried chili flakes**

2 ounces (57g) **butter**

1 **large lemon**, juiced

½ cup (30g) chopped **fresh parsley**

Salt and pepper to season

NUTRITONAL FACTS
per serve

Calories 233, Fat 13.5g, Carbohydrate 3.3g, Dietary Fiber 0.7g, Net Carbs 2.6g, Protein 24.4g

CHILI CHICKEN SKEWERS

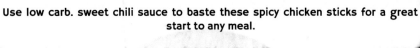

Use low carb. sweet chili sauce to baste these spicy chicken sticks for a great start to any meal.

INGREDIENTS

2 pounds (908g) **chicken breast meat**, cubed

½ cup (119ml) **olive oil**

7 cloves **garlic**, finely chopped

½ cup (8g) **cilantro**, chopped

2 tbsp. **white vinegar**

1 **large red chili** (to taste), finely chopped

3 tbsp. **powdered sugar substitute**

Salt and pepper to season

Serves 6

DIRECTIONS

In a small bowl mix together the oil, 6 of the garlic cloves and the cilantro.

Season with salt and pepper.

Place the chicken cubes in a large bowl and cover them with the cilantro marinade. Ensure they are well covered, use your hands if necessary.

Cover and place in the refrigerator for several hours or even overnight.

While the chicken is marinating, make the sweet chili sauce.

In a small sauce pan heat together the vinegar and sugar substitute. Add the extra clove of garlic and the chili pepper.

Simmer gently for a couple of minutes.

Pour into a small bowl to cool.

When you are ready to cook the chicken pre-heat a griddle to medium.

Thread the chicken onto skewers and place on the hot griddle and cook, turning frequently for 10 – 15 minutes until cooked through.

As the Skewers are cooking baste them with the chili sauce.

Be careful they do not burn but only turn a glazed golden brown.

Remove from the heat and serve while still hot.

NUTRITONAL FACTS
per serve

Calories 339, Fat 20.6g, Carbohydrate 5.4g, Dietary Fiber 0.2g, Net Carbs 5.2g, Protein 32.3g

SAUCY BEEF BALLS

Serves 6

Serve these beef balls in small individual bowls so that everyone can get a taste of the distinctive sauce that they are cooked in.

DIRECTIONS

In a large bowl, mix together the beef, shallots, 2 cloves garlic, bell pepper, cheese, olive oil and the egg.

Season to taste and using wet hands form the mixture into 48 small balls.

Heat some olive oil in a large skillet and fry the meat balls until nicely brown on all sides.

Drain from the oil and place in a large saucepan.

When all of the meat balls are brown and in the saucepan mix together all the rest of the ingredients (except for the garnish), for the sauce.

Pour over the meat balls and place the sauce pan over a low heat on top of the stove.

Slowly bring to the boil as you do not want to burn the meat or the sauce.

Turn the heat right down and simmer for 20 – 25 minutes until the sauce has reduced and is coating the meat.

Remove from the heat and serve in individual bowls.

Top with chopped or sliced green onions.

INGREDIENTS

1½ pounds (681g) **ground beef**

3 **shallots**, finely chopped

5 cloves **garlic**, finely chopped

1 **small red bell pepper**, seeded and finely chopped

1 **large fresh egg**

3 tbsp. **Cheddar cheese**, shredded

1 tbsp. **olive oil**

½ cup (119ml) **light soy sauce**

½ cup (119ml) **water**

1 tbsp. **granulated sugar substitute**

1 tsp. **chili sauce** (to taste)

1 tbsp. **tomato paste**

1 tbsp. **rice wine vinegar**

Olive oil for frying

Salt and pepper to season

Green onions to garnish

NUTRITONAL FACTS
per serve

Calories 319, Fat 14.6g, Carbohydrate 5.8g, Dietary Fiber 0.4g, Net Carbs 5.4g, Protein 38.2g

TANGY SALMON BURGERS

These little burgers are baked in the oven and are very easy to make. Use fresh salmon or really well drained tinned salmon, (or even tuna). Serve with some mayonnaise flavored with a little wasabi paste and some slices of avocado.

INGREDIENTS

1½ pounds (681g) **fresh salmon fillet**

1 cup (237ml) **unsweetened almond milk** to poach the salmon

1 tbsp. **butter**

2 tbsp. **light soy sauce**

3 **green onions**, minced

½ inch (1.3cm) **fresh green ginger**, grated

½ tsp. **wasabi paste**

2 **fresh eggs**, beaten

3 tbsp. **coconut flour**

Salt and pepper to season

Serves 6

DIRECTIONS

Heat the milk and the butter in a skillet large enough to hold the salmon, over a medium high heat.

Cut the salmon into chunks and add it to the hot milk and butter.

Simmer the fish in the milk for 10 – 15 minutes until it flakes easily. Do not overcook.

Remove the fish from the heat and take it out of the milk. Drain and leave to cool.

When cool, flake the salmon, removing any skin and bones.

Place the flakes in a medium sized bowl.

Mix together the soy sauce, green onion, ginger, and wasabi paste and fork it through the salmon.

Mix in the beaten eggs.

Season to taste.

Mix in the coconut flour.

Form into 12 patties using slightly damp hands and place them on a parchment lined baking tray.

Cover with cling film and refrigerate for 30 minutes.

Pre-heat the oven to 400°F.

Remove the salmon cakes from the fridge and place in the hot oven.

Cook for 12 – 15 minutes until heated completely through.

Serve.

NUTRITONAL FACTS
per serve

Calories 260, Fat 15.8g, Carbohydrate 4.6g
Dietary Fiber 1.7g, Net Carbs 2.9g, Protein 24.6g

SHRIMP CEVICHE

Serves 4

Modern and trendy, shrimp ceviche will be a great starter for your next dinner party. Use lime juice if you can or lemon juice makes a very acceptable variation. Twist the salmon strips into roses for an attractive serve.

DIRECTIONS

Place the shrimp in a glass or ceramic bowl.

Cover the shrimp with the lime juice and leave it for 8 – 10 minutes until it turns pink and opaque.

Stir a couple of times to ensure the even distribution of the lime juice.

Place the shallot, cucumber, tomato, jalapeno and avocado into a large glass bowl and very gently toss together.

Drain the shrimp from the lime juice using a wooden or plastic spoon and place it into the vegetables.

Toss gently.

Season with salt and pepper and the herb of choice and then pour over the remaining lime juice that was used to marinade the shrimp.

Cover the dish with plastic cling film and refrigerate for 45 minutes to an hour to allow the flavors to mingle.

Serve with the sliced bell pepper, salmon strips and lime wedges.

INGREDIENTS

1 pound (454g) **medium shrimp**, cleaned weight

1 cup (237ml) **lime juice**

1 **large shallot**, finely diced

½ **cucumber**, seeded and chopped

1 **jalapeno pepper**, seeded and finely chopped (to taste)

2 **avocados**, peeled and diced

2 tbsp. **fresh cilantro or parsley**, chopped

1 **tomato**, diced

Salt and pepper to season

½ **red bell pepper**, seeded and finely sliced

6 ounces (170g) **smoked salmon strips**

Lime wedges

NUTRITONAL FACTS
per serve

Calories 388, Fat 22.9g, Carbohydrate 15.0g, Dietary Fiber 8.0g, Net Carbs 7.0g, Protein 34.3g

BACON & BROCCOLI SOUP

A creamy, cheesy broccoli soup with the scrumptious addition of smoky bacon.
Such a body warming dish, perfect for a cold day.

Serves 6

DIRECTIONS

In a large saucepan melt the butter and fry the chopped bacon until crispy.

Add the shallot and garlic and continue to cook until the shallot becomes translucent.

Add the broth and the cream cheese and stir well until nicely blended.

Add the broccoli and cook for 8 – 10 minutes over a low heat until the broccoli is tender.

Break up the broccoli a little with a fork if it is too bulky.

Add the cheeses, cream and pepper.

Simmer over a low heat until heated through – do not let the soup boil.

Liquidise or process until smooth.

Serve in warm bowls with a piece of broccoli in each dish.

INGREDIENTS

4 tbsp. **butter**

2 cloves **garlic**, finely chopped

1 **medium shallot**, finely chopped

4 cups (948ml) **vegetable broth**

4 tbsp. **cream cheese**

3 cups (273g) **broccoli**, chopped (save 6 sprigs for serve)

4 ounces (113g) **Cheddar cheese**, shredded

8 ounces (227g) **Gruyere cheese**, shredded

4 tbsp. **heavy cream**

6 ounces (170g) **smoky bacon**, very finely chopped

Pepper to season

NUTRITONAL FACTS
per serve

Calories 465, Fat 37.5g, Carbohydrate 4.8g, Dietary Fiber 1.2g, Net Carbs 3.6g, Protein 27.7g

LEMONY CHICKEN SOUP

Serves 4

Try this creamy chicken soup with a lemon tang.
The addition of the cheese gives it extra body and a really unique flavor.

DIRECTIONS

Place the chicken serves in a large saucepan with the broth, shallot, garlic, bay leaf, thyme and oregano.

Bring to the boil over a medium high heat.

Add the lemon slices and some seasoning.

Cover the saucepan and turn the heat down to a simmer.

Simmer for 40 – 45 minutes until the chicken is cooked.

Remove from the heat and take the chicken out, placing it in a bowl to cool enough to handle.

Strain the cooking liquid into a clean saucepan, discarding the vegetables and herbs.

Remove the chicken from the bone and leave in chunky pieces.

Add the wine, cheese, cream and the chicken to the liquid in the saucepan.

Stir well together. Check the seasoning.

Heat everything together over a low heat until piping hot.

Do not let the soup boil.

Serve in warm bowls with half of an egg.

INGREDIENTS

3 **chicken leg serves**, skinned and cut into thighs and drumsticks

5 cups (1.2L) **chicken broth**

1 **shallot**, chopped

2 cloves **garlic**, crushed

1 **bay leaf**, bruised

1 sprig **fresh thyme**

1 sprig **fresh oregano**

1 **small lemon**, thinly sliced

¼ cup (59ml) **dry white wine**

½ cup (57g) **Pecorino cheese**, finely shredded

½ cup (118ml) **heavy cream**

Salt and pepper to season

2 **fresh eggs**, hard boiled, peeled and halved

NUTRITONAL FACTS
per serve

Calories 342, Fat 18.5g, Carbohydrate 4.6g, Dietary Fiber 0.6g, Net Carbs 4.0g, Protein 35.9g

MUSHROOM SOUP

Mushroom soup is an all-time favorite and this one is creamy, hearty, warming and filling fare.
Try it as a starter to a meal or at any time of the day for a quick 'pick me up'.

Serves 6

DIRECTIONS

Melt the butter in a large saucepan over a medium heat.

Sauté the shallot and garlic for a couple of minutes.

Add the sliced mushrooms and stir-fry until nice and buttery.

Add the broth, wine, thyme and seasoning.

Cover and simmer for 30 minutes.

Stir in the cream.

Reheat gently until piping hot. Do not boil.

Serve in warm bowls.

INGREDIENTS

8 tbsp. **butter**

1¼ pounds (568g) **cremini mushrooms**, wiped and sliced

1 **large shallot**, finely chopped

2 cloves **garlic**, finely chopped

3 cups (711ml) **chicken broth**

2 cups (473ml) **heavy cream**

¼ cup (59ml) **dry white wine**

2 tsp. **fresh thyme**, finely chopped

Salt and pepper to season

NUTRITONAL FACTS
per serve

Calories 330, Fat 30.9g, Carbohydrate 6.6g, Dietary Fiber 0.7g, Net Carbs 5.9g, Protein 5.9g

MEXICAN STUFFED BELL PEPPERS

Serves 6

These peppers form a fairly substantial starter to a meal. They are great as a snack too, and would also make a superb luncheon dish. Use different colors of peppers for a fun presentation.

DIRECTIONS

Pre-heat the oven to 375°F (191°C).

Cut the tops off the peppers, scoop out the seeds, and trim the bases so they peppers stand upright.

Place the peppers in a small, deep baking dish, cut side up.

Chop the pepper you have cut off into a small dice and set aside.

Heat the oil in a large skillet over a medium high heat.

Sauté the onion, chopped pepper and the garlic until the onion is soft and translucent.

Add the beef and the chorizo to the skillet and fry until nicely brown and separated.

Stir in the chopped tomato, tomato paste, mozzarella, herbs, Tobasco and seasoning.

Mix everything well together.

Spoon the meat mixture into the pepper cases.

Sprinkle the pecorino cheese on top.

Cover the dish with foil and place in the hot oven.

Bake for 30 – 40 minutes.

Remove the foil and continue baking for 15 more minutes until the tops are brown and the pecorino melted.

Serve hot with the sliced avocado on the side.

NUTRITONAL FACTS
per serve

Calories 485, Fat 28.0g, Carbohydrate 14.1g, Dietary Fiber 5.4g, Net Carbs 8.7g, Protein 44.5g

INGREDIENTS

6 **medium to large bell peppers**

12 ounces (340g) **ground beef**

12 ounces (340g) **ground chorizo**

½ **small onion,** finely chopped

3 cloves **garlic,** finely chopped

½ cup (121g) chopped **tinned tomatoes**

1 tsp. **powdered chili**

2 tsp. **powdered cumin**

½ tsp. **dried oregano**

2 tbsp. **tomato paste**

1½ cups (170g) shredded **mozzarella cheese**

½ cup (57g) grated **Pecorino cheese**

3 tbsp. **olive oil**

Few drops **Tabasco**

Salt and pepper to season

Slices of **avocado** to serve

MAC & CHEESE NUGGETS

Keto macaroni alias cauliflower takes on a different guise in these cheese nuggets. Monterey Jack cheese may be used instead of Cheshire in this recipe. Serve them with a slice of avocado and some crispy watercress.

INGREDIENTS

1 **large head cauliflower**, broken into florets

6 ounces (170g) **Cheshire cheese**

1 tsp. **powdered garlic**

1 tsp. **powdered onion**

3 **medium fresh eggs**, beaten

1 **large fresh egg**

¼ cup (59ml) **unsweetened almond milk**

1 cup (70g) coarsely crushed **pork rinds**

Salt and freshly ground black pepper to season

Serves 6

DIRECTIONS

Cook the cauliflower in some salted water until tender – do not let it become mushy.

Drain very well. Pat dry with a paper towel and spread out on an open plate for 30 minutes to finish drying.

Pre-heat the oven to 375°F (191°C).

Prepare a baking sheet by covering it with parchment paper.

Place the dry cauliflower in a processor and pulse until it looks like breadcrumbs.

Place the cauliflower in a large bowl and stir in the cheese, garlic and onion powder and seasoning to taste.

Stir in the beaten eggs, using enough to give a stiff mixture.

Beat the large egg and milk together in a shallow bowl.

Place the pork rinds on a plate.

Divide the cauliflower mixture into 12 serves and form small nuggets with damp hands.

Place each nugget in the egg mixture and roll in the pork rinds.

Carefully place on the prepared baking sheet.

Bake for 20 – 25 minutes in the hot oven until nicely golden and crisp.

Serve hot.

NUTRITONAL FACTS
per serve

Calories 236, Fat 15.0g, Carbohydrate 9.1g, Dietary Fiber 3.5g, Net Carbs 5.6g, Protein 18.9g

AVOCADO CHIPS

Serves 6

Crisp chips with a melting centre. Easily made in the oven when avocados are in season – oh and completely addictive too so be warned – the calories and carbs can add up if serving sizes start getting ignored.

DIRECTIONS

Pre-heat the oven to 420°F (216°C).

Prepare a large roasting tin by lining it with parchment.

Mix the coconut flour with the salt on a large plate.

Beat the eggs in a large shallow bowl.

Mix together the pork crackling and garlic on a large plate.

Dip the avocado slices in the coconut flour.

Dip them in the egg and finally toss in the pork crackling.

Place in the prepared roasting pan.

Sprinkle with olive oil.

Cook in the hot oven for 25 - 30 minutes until brown and crisp.

Remove from the oven and carefully place on a serve plate.

Sprinkle with Parmesan cheese.

Serve hot with a dip of sour cream mixed with lime juice.

INGREDIENTS

½ cup (56g) **coconut flour**

2 tsp. **salt**

2 **large fresh eggs**, beaten

2 cups (140g) **pork rinds**, crushed

3 cloves **garlic**, finely chopped

3 **firm ripe avocados**, peeled and cut into wedges

Olive oil

Grated **Parmesan cheese** to serve

¾ cup (178ml) **sour cream** to serve

1 **lime**, juiced, to serve

NUTRITONAL FACTS
per serve

Calories 461, Fat 38.5g, Carbohydrate 16.2g, Dietary Fiber 10.1g, Net Carbs 6.1g, Protein 15.8g

MEATY MUSHROOMS

Thank the almighty mushroom Gods for their shape that we can stuff them with pepperoni and cheese.
Top with extra cheese if you feel the urge, and even a dash of Tabasco sauce.

INGREDIENTS

18 **large mushrooms**

6 ounces (170g) **pepperoni**, finely chopped

1 **small onion**, finely chopped

5 cloves **garlic**, finely chopped

1 tbsp. **olive oil**

1 **egg**

6 ounces (170g) **cream cheese**

¼ cup (59ml) **plain Greek yogurt**

4 ounces (113g) **Gruyere cheese**, shredded

⅓ cup (78ml) **dry white wine**

1 tbsp. freshly chopped **parsley**

Salt and pepper to taste

Serves 6

DIRECTIONS

Pre-heat the oven to 375°F (191°C).

Wipe the mushrooms, carefully remove the stalks and place the caps, top side down in a large, greased oven proof dish.

Chop the stems finely.

Heat a large skillet over a medium high heat. Add the oil and sauté the onion, garlic and mushroom stems until soft.

Remove the onion mixture and place it in a large bowl to cool a little.

Add the wine to the pan and deglaze it. Add this liquid to the onions.

Mix the pepperoni into the onions.

Spoon into the mushroom cups.

Beat together the cream cheese, yogurt, cheese, seasoning and parsley.

Add the egg and mix well together.

Spoon the mixture evenly over the pepperoni/onion mixture.

Place in the hot oven and bake for 20 – 25 minutes until hot and bubbly.

Remove from the oven and leave to cool for a few minutes before serve.

NUTRITONAL FACTS
per serve

Calories 382, Fat 31.7g, Carbohydrate 5.1g, Dietary Fiber 0.5g, Net Carbs 4.6g, Protein 16.7g

HAM ROLL-UPS

Makes 16

These are perfect for a light starter or even to serve as appetisers at a party.

DIRECTIONS

Lay the ham slices out on a flat surface.

Beat together the cream cheese and the chili sauce.

Spread the cheese over the ham slices.

Sprinkle each slice with a small amount of chopped onion.

Place the dill quarters along the top edge of each slice of ham and roll up from the pickle end.

Secure with toothpicks.

Refrigerate, covered so that the ham does not dry out until ready to serve.

Remove from the refrigerator and cut each roll in half with a sharp knife.

Serve.

INGREDIENTS

8 **slices ham**, thinly sliced

¾ cup (174g) **cream cheese**

1 tsp. **chili sauce**

4 **long dill pickles**, sliced lengthwise into quarters

2 **pickled onions**, finely chopped

16 **toothpicks**

NUTRITONAL FACTS
per roll-up

Calories 63, Fat 5.0g, Carbohydrate 1.2g, Dietary Fiber 0.4g, Net Carbs 0.8g, Protein 3.2g

MAINS

PULLED PORK WITH BARBEQUE SAUCE

An amazing, superbly tender way of cooking a pork roast;
the pork will fall apart once it is cooked but if left to cool will slice quite happily
with a sharp knife.

Serves 8

DIRECTIONS

Pre-heat the oven to 400°F (204°C).

In a small bowl, mix together the powdered chili, garlic, onion, black pepper and salt.

Rub this mixture all over the pork shoulder and place it in a roasting pan, large enough to fit it comfortably.

Place in the oven and roast for 1¼ hours.

Reduce the oven temperature to 300°F (149°C).

Remove the pork from the oven and pour off any excess fat.

Pour the root beer around the pork.

Cover tightly with foil and return to the oven for another 2½ to 3 hours until the meat is tender.

While the pork continues to cook make a barbeque sauce by mixing together all of the remaining ingredients in a medium sized saucepan.

Place over a medium heat and bring to the boil.

Reduce the heat to a simmer and cook uncovered until thickened, about 12 – 15 minutes.

Remove the pork from the oven when cooked.

Take the foil off and shred the meat using two forks.

Mix the pork with the barbeque sauce and serve.

INGREDIENTS

Pork:

4 pounds (1.8kg) **boneless pork shoulder** in 1 piece, skinless

1 tsp. **powdered chili**

1 tsp. **powdered garlic**

1 tsp. **powdered onion**

½ tsp. **black pepper**

1 tsp. **salt**

2 cups (474ml) **sugar free root beer or ginger beer**

Sauce:

6 **green onions**, chopped

4 cloves **garlic**, finely chopped

⅓ cup (78ml) **olive oil**

¼ cup (50g) **granulated sugar substitute**

2 tsp. **powdered mustard**

1 tsp. **powdered paprika**

2 cups (474ml) **water**

½ cup (119ml) **cider vinegar**

2 tbsp. **Worcestershire sauce**

2 **jalapeño chilies**, seeded and chopped (to taste)

4 tbsp. **tomato paste**

NUTRITONAL FACTS
per serve

Calories 687, Fat 55.4g, Carbohydrate 4.9g, Dietary Fiber 0.9g, Net Carbs 4.0g, Protein 39.0g

CHEESY BACON PIE

Serves 6

DIRECTIONS

Pre-heat the oven to 300°F (149°C).

Grease a deep 12 inch (30cm) pie plate with butter.

Heat the olive oil in a large skillet over a medium high heat.

Sauté the chopped shallots until translucent. Drain and place in a small dish.

In the same skillet fry the beef and bacon until brown, Break up any lumps and mix well together.

Drain any extra fat off the mince mixture and add the shallots.

Stir in the Cheddar cheese, season with pepper and spoon into the pie plate.

Place the mayonnaise, cream and eggs into a medium sized bowl and whisk well together. Season with pepper.

Pour this mixture over the meat.

Sprinkle the Gruyere cheese on top.

Place the dish in the pre-heated oven and bake for 25 – 30 minutes until nicely browned.

Remove from the oven and sprinkle the top with cayenne pepper.

NUTRITONAL FACTS
per serve

Calories 738, Fat 62.2g, Carbohydrate 2.1g, Dietary Fiber 0g, Net Carbs 2.1g, Protein 42.1g

Beef and bacon mix to make a tasty pie, topped with a cheesy egg custard. Serve with green vegetables or let the pie cool a little and serve with a green crunchy salad. This can also be made in individual casserole dishes.

INGREDIENTS

¾ pound (341g) **ground beef**

¾ pound (341g) **ground bacon**

4 **small shallots**, finely diced

1 tbsp. **olive oil**

2 **large fresh eggs**

¾ cup (178ml) **creamy mayonnaise**

⅓ cup (79ml) **heavy cream**

6 ounces (170g) **Cheddar or Colby cheese**, shredded

6 ounces (170g) **Gruyere cheese**, shredded

Powdered cayenne pepper to sprinkle

Butter to grease

Pepper to season

POT ROASTED BEEF

This is a succulent way to cook a cheaper cut of beef.
This dish could also be made in a slow cooker, if you have one.

Serves 8

NUTRITONAL FACTS
per serve

Calories 734, Fat 54.0g, Carbohydrate 4.5g,
Dietary Fiber 0.3g, Net Carbs 4.2g, Protein 53.4g

INGREDIENTS

3 pounds (1.4kg) **beef, chuck or a round of beef**

1 **onion**, coarsely chopped

1 **head of garlic** cut in half horizontally

6 **rashers bacon**, chopped

1 cup (237ml) **beef broth**

2 tbsp. **Worcestershire sauce**

3 tbsp. **red wine vinegar**

2 tsp. **hot ready-made mustard**

2 tbsp. **granulated sugar substitute**

2 large sprigs **fresh thyme**

Salt and pepper to season

DIRECTIONS

Pre-heat the oven to 350°F (177°C).

Heat a large skillet over a medium high heat and add the bacon.

Sauté the bacon until the fat begins to run and it is cooked but not crisp.

Add the onion and sauté until translucent. Set aside.

Season the beef with salt and pepper and brown it on all sides in the skillet.

Place the browned beef in a large casserole dish that has a lid.

Add the onions, bacon and the 2 pieces of garlic head.

Mix together the broth, Worcestershire sauce, vinegar, mustard and sugar substitute.

Pour this liquid over the beef. Add a sprig of thyme either side of the beef.

Cover with the casserole dish with the lid and place in the hot oven.

Cook for 2½ – 3 hours until the meat is tender.

When cooked, lift the meat out of the juices and the casserole and place on a plate. Cover with foil and allow to rest for 15 minutes.

Skim off any extra fat in the casserole, remove the thyme and squeeze the garlic to remove the flesh from the skins. Discard the thyme and garlic skins.

Reduce sauce if liked, and serve in a separate dish.

Slice and serve with green seasonal vegetables.

HAM AND BEEF LASAGNA

Serves 6

I love lasagne. This was not easy for me to say goodbye to. So, I didn't. Layers of beef, ham, bacon and creamy cheese sauce are the perfect tasty Keto alternative, and keep those cravings under control and guilt free.

DIRECTIONS

Pre-heat the oven to 375°F (191°C).

Grease a deep 12 inch (30cm) pie dish with butter.

Heat the oil in a large skillet over a medium high heat.

Sauté the onion and the garlic until tender.

Add the ground beef and bacon and stir until brown all over. Break up any lumps as you go.

When the meat is brown add the tomato paste, chopped herbs, red wine and the broth.

Cook gently over a low heat until well blended. Season to taste.

Remove from the heat and set aside.

Beat together the sour cream and heavy cream. Season to taste.

Place one third of the meat mixture into the prepared dish.

Cover with a layer of ham.

Spoon over ½ cup (119ml) of the creamy sauce.

Sprinkle with 2 ounces (56g) of cheese.

Repeat these layers twice more ending with cheese on the top.

Place the lasagne in the hot oven and bake for 25 – 30 minutes until bubbly and brown on the top.

Serve.

INGREDIENTS

1¼ pounds (568g) **ground beef**

3 **slices bacon**, finely chopped

1½ tbsp. **tomato paste**

1 **large onion**, finely chopped

3 cloves **garlic**, finely chopped

1 tbsp. **butter**

1 tbsp. **olive oil**

1 tsp. **fresh thyme**, finely chopped

1 tsp. **fresh parsley**, finely chopped

¼ cup (59ml) **dry red wine**

¼ cup (59ml) **beef broth**

12 **slices ham**

1 cup (237ml) **sour cream**

½ cup (118ml) **heavy cream**

7 ounces (198g) **mozzarella cheese**

Salt and pepper to season

NUTRITONAL FACTS
per serve

Calories 630, Fat 46.9g, Carbohydrate 9.3g, Dietary Fiber 1.5g, Net Carbs 7.8g, Protein 41.4g

SPICED LAMB CHOPS & GUACAMOLE

An enticing and simple way to cook lamb chops. They may be cooked in a skillet and in the oven or over the barbeque.
Serve with guacamole and a green salad.

INGREDIENTS

12 **meaty lamb loin chops**

2 tbsp. **olive oil**

6 cloves **garlic**, grated

3 tsp. **fresh thyme**, finely chopped

½ tsp. **powdered chili**

1 **lemon**, zest only

1 tsp. freshly ground **black pepper**

1 tbsp. **olive oil**

Salt to season

Guacamole:

3 **medium ripe avocados**

1 **medium red onion**, very finely diced

1 tbsp. **fresh lime juice**

½ tsp. **salt**

1 tbsp. **dried red pepper flakes**

Fresh cilantro, finely chopped (to taste)

Serves 6

DIRECTIONS

Pre-heat the oven to 375°F (191°C).

In a small bowl combine the olive oil, garlic, thyme, chili, lemon zest, and pepper and salt to taste.

Mix well to a spicy paste.

Rub the chops well with the spice mix.

Heat a large non-stick skillet over a high heat, add the olive oil and brown the chops on all sides for 5 minutes.

Continue to cook in the skillet on top of the stove or place the chops in the oven to complete cooking.

Leave in the oven for 8 – 10 minutes. Check the chops so that they are cooked how you prefer them.

Serve hot.

While the chops are cooking make the guacamole.

Peel, pip and mash the avocado.

Beat in the onion, lime juice, salt and red pepper flakes.

Stir in some chopped cilantro to taste.

Refrigerate until used.

NUTRITONAL FACTS - Lamb Chops
per serve

Calories 539, Fat 45.4g, Carbohydrate 1.7g, Dietary Fiber 0.4g, Net Carbs 1.3g, Protein 28.3g

NUTRITONAL FACTS - Guacamole
per serve

Calories 165, Fat 14.8g, Carbohydrate 9.3g, Dietary Fiber 5.7g, Net Carbs 3.6g, Protein 1.7g

BAKED TEXAN CHICKEN

Serves 6

DIRECTIONS

Trim the chicken wings.

In a small bowl, mix together the garlic, paprika, thyme, salt and pepper.

Rub this mixture into the chicken using your hands.

Place in a ceramic or glass dish, cover with cling film and refrigerate for 4 hours.

When you are ready to cook the chicken, pre-heat the oven to 375°F (191°C).

Fry the bacon in a small skillet until crispy.

Cool and crumble. Set aside.

Have ready a large non-stick roasting tin.

Remove the chicken from the fridge and spoon off any extra liquid that may have settled.

Pat the chicken dry with paper towel.

Mix the crumbled bacon with the coconut flour.

Beat the eggs in a flat dish with some seasoning.

Coat the chicken with egg and toss them in the bacon and flour, making sure all of the pieces are well coated.

Heat some oil in a large skillet over a medium high heat.

Add the chicken pieces to the skillet a few at a time and quickly fry them until a golden brown on the surface.

Drain the pieces and place them in the roasting tin.

Place the chicken in the hot oven and continue to cook it for 30 – 35 minutes.

Test that it is done by inserting a sharp knife near the bone – the juices should run clear.

When cooked, remove from the oven and serve.

Flavors abound in this tempting recipe, good for a family and also easily increased for a crowd – and what a crowd pleaser it is!
Supply lots of paper napkins for finger licking goodness.

NUTRITONAL FACTS
per serve

Calories 697, Fat 45.4g, Carbohydrate 10.9g, Dietary Fiber 6.7g, Net Carbs 4.2g, Protein 58.5g

INGREDIENTS

3½ pounds (1.6kg) **chicken thighs and drumsticks**, mixed

1 tsp. **powdered garlic**

1½ tsp. **powdered paprika**

1 tsp. **fresh thyme**, finely chopped

1 cup (112g) **coconut flour**

2 **large eggs**, beaten

4 **slices bacon**

Salt and pepper to season

Oil for browning

PORTOBELLO BUN HAMBURGERS

No bun, instead a delicious mushroom, but nevertheless a burger!
Enjoy the juicy goodness topped with an additional slice of cheese, onion rings
and crisp lettuce. A sugar free tomato sauce is also a welcome addition.

INGREDIENTS

2 pounds (908g) **ground beef**, not extra lean

4 ounces (113g) **bacon**, ground

2 cloves **garlic**, finely diced

1 **large onion**, finely diced

1 tbsp. **soy sauce**

1 tsp. **dried parsley**

2 ounces (57g) **Cheddar cheese**, cut into 8 cubes

4 tbsp. **olive oil**

12 **large portobello mushroom caps**

Salt and pepper to season

Serves 6

DIRECTIONS

Heat 2 tablespoons of oil in a large skillet over a medium high heat.

Sautee the onion and garlic until the onion is tender, about 5 minutes.

Remove the onion from the heat and cool a little.

In a large bowl, mix together the ground meats, soy sauce, parsley, salt and pepper and the onions.

Divide the meat mixture into 6 even serves and flatten each to form a burger.

Press a cube of cheese into the center of each burger and seal it inside by pressing the meat mixture around it.

Reform the burger patty if necessary.

Heat the remaining oil in a clean skillet and fry the burger patties on both sides until nicely browned and cooked through.

When cooked, drain on a paper towel. Keep warm.

Sauté the mushrooms in the same skillet for a couple of minutes until tender.

Sandwich each patty inside two mushroom halves.

Serve whilst still warm with green vegetables of your choice or just as they are topped with extra cheese and onion.

NUTRITONAL FACTS
per burger

Calories 571, Fat 42.8g, Carbohydrate 10.2g, Dietary Fiber 2.7g, Net Carbs 7.5g, Protein 39.6g

SWEET & SOUR CHICKEN

Serves 4

DIRECTIONS

Pre-heat the oven to 350°F (177°C).

Cover a shallow roasting tray with parchment paper.

Chop the chicken breasts into even sized pieces.

In a bowl mix together the powdered pork rind, almond flour, salt and pepper.

In a small bowl beat the eggs.

Heat the olive oil in a large skillet over a medium high heat.

Dip the chicken pieces into the egg and then into the almond flour mix. Toss well to coat.

Fry the chicken pieces quickly in the hot oil until nicely browned.

Drain on paper towel and place on the roasting try.

When all of the chicken is brown put them in the hot oven and cook for 20 – 25 minutes until cooked through.

Meanwhile place all of the other ingredients except for the arrowroot powder, water and sesame seeds into a small sauce pan and bring to the boil.

Reduce the heat to a simmer and continue to cook for 5 minutes more.

Mix the arrowroot powder with the cold water. Add a couple of spoonfuls of the hot sauce to the arrowroot and mix well.

Add the arrowroot to the sauce and stir to thicken.

When the chicken is cooked, remove it from the oven and place it in a serve bowl.

Pour over the sweet and sour sauce and sprinkle with sesame seeds.

Serve.

Tasty little chicken pieces in a sweet and sour sauce give a wonderful authenticity to this Chinese favorite.

INGREDIENTS

5 **chicken breast serves**, boned and skinned

2 **large fresh eggs**

¾ cup (53g) **pork rinds**, powdered

¾ cup (72g) **almond flour**

½ cup (119ml) **rice wine vinegar**

½ cup (119ml) **chicken broth**

⅔ cup (132g) **granulated sugar substitute**

1 tsp. **ginger root**, freshly grated

1 **small green pepper**, seeded and finely chopped

3 tbsp. **soy sauce**

2 tsp. **powdered arrowroot**

1 tbsp. **water**

3 tbsp. **olive oil**

Salt and pepper to season

Sesame seeds to sprinkle

NUTRITONAL FACTS
per serve

Calories 695, Fat 37.1g, Carbohydrate 9.5g, Dietary Fiber 2.9g, Net Carbs 6.7g, Protein 75.1g

SUNNY STUFFED CHICKEN BREASTS

A perfect treat for the whole family! Chicken breasts just oozing rich, lush cheese and filling your home with a fantastic smell.

Serves 6

INGREDIENTS

6 **chicken breasts**, skinned and boned

½ cup (124g) **ricotta cheese**

½ cup (54g) **Gruyere cheese**, finely shredded

1 tsp. **fresh thyme**, finely chopped

1 tsp. **fresh parsley**, finely chopped

½ cup (55g) **sundried tomatoes in olive oil**, diced

12 **baby spinach leaves**, torn

6 slices **mozzarella cheese** (optional)

Salt and pepper to season

Powdered paprika to garnish

DIRECTIONS

Pre-heat the oven to 375°F (191°C).

Carefully slice open each chicken breast, with a sharp knife, to make a pocket in each one.

Have ready an ovenproof dish large enough to hold the chicken breasts, side by side.

In a medium sized bowl mix together the rest of the ingredients except the mozzarella cheese and the garnish.

Divide the cheese mixture into 6 and spoon each serve into the pockets made in the chicken breasts.

Secure each opening with one or two toothpicks to hold the filling inside.

Lay the chicken breasts into the dish and top each one with a slice of mozzarella cheese if using.

Place the dish in the hot oven and bake for 35 - 40 minutes uncovered.

Check that the chicken is cooked and brown on the top.

Serve.

NUTRITONAL FACTS
per serve

Calories 401, Fat 16.5g, Carbohydrate 5.2g, Dietary Fiber 1.0g, Net Carbs 4.2g, Protein 55.4g

BEEF STIR-FRY

Serves 6

DIRECTIONS

Heat the oil in a large skillet or wok over a high heat.

Add the onions and stir fry for a few minutes until translucent.

Add the bell pepper, broccoli and the mushrooms and fry for a minute or so.

Add the beef steak and fry until it is brown.

Stir in the cabbage and toss everything together.

Pour over the soy sauce, sprinkle the spice and sambal oelek over the dish and mix everything together well.

Season with salt and pepper.

Serve whilst still hot and the vegetables remain crispy.

NUTRITONAL FACTS
per serve

Calories 239, Fat 12.5g, Carbohydrate 15.4g, Dietary Fiber 5.5g, Net Carbs 9.9g, Protein 19.6g

A quick and easy dish to prepare for dinner after a long day at work. To save time the vegetables could be prepared in the morning and kept covered in the fridge.

INGREDIENTS

2 tbsp. **olive oil**

1 **large onion**, finely sliced

1 **large bell pepper**, seeded and sliced

10 ounces (284g) **portobello mushrooms**, sliced

1 **small green cabbage**, coarsely shredded

8 ounces (227g) **small broccoli florets**

1 pound (454g) **rump or fillet steak**, sliced into thin strips

2 tbsp. **light soy sauce**

2 tsp. **powdered Chinese five spice**

1 tsp. **sambal oelek or chili sauce**

Salt and pepper to season

SPICY BEEF CURRY

A curry is a great dish to enjoy on a Keto diet. As with all curries this one is still yummy the next day so plan ahead and make a double quantity as it freezes well. Try serving this with cauliflower rice.

INGREDIENTS

1½ pounds (681g) **beef chuck steak**, cubed

1 **large onion**, chopped

3 cloves **garlic**, chopped

1 inch (2.5cm) piece **green ginger**, grated

2 tbsp. **powdered coriander**

½ tsp. **mustard seeds**

1 tsp. **powdered cumin**

1 tsp. **powdered chili** (to taste)

1 stick **cinnamon bark**

1 tsp. **garam masala**

2 tbsp. **olive oil**

1 cup (237ml) **water**

Chopped cilantro to garnish

Salt and pepper to season

Serves 6

DIRECTIONS

Heat the oil in a large skillet over a medium high heat.

Add the onion and sauté until it becomes translucent.

Add the garlic and the ginger and sauté for a minute more.

Add all of the spices and sauté until they become fragrant.

Add the beef to the skillet and fry until it is brown and nicely covered in the spice mixture.

Spoon everything into a large saucepan.

Add the water and season to taste.

Cook over a low heat for 1 – 1½ hours until the beef is tender.

Cook for longer if necessary.

Adjust the seasoning when the curry is ready and serve sprinkled with chopped cilantro.

NUTRITONAL FACTS
per serve

Calories 460, Fat 34.3g, Carbohydrate 5.2g, Dietary Fiber 2.2g, Net Carbs 3.0g, Protein 31.1g

GINGER SOY SALMON

Serves 6

DIRECTIONS

Cut the salmon into 6 pieces.

Place in a shallow heatproof glass or ceramic dish side by side.

Mix together the rest of the ingredients except the sesame seeds.

Pour half of it over the salmon and gently rub it in to the fish.

Cover with cling film and refrigerate for half an hour.

Meanwhile turn on a broiler to high.

Remove the salmon from the fridge and broil for 10 minutes.

Turn the salmon over and top with the rest of the chili mixture and broil for a few minutes longer.

The cooking time will depend on the thickness of the fish fillets but do not overcook. The fish should not be pink when cooked and should flake easily.

Serve the individual serves on plates and sprinkle each piece with some toasted sesame seeds.

Exquisite fresh salmon chunks with a tangy sauce.
Eat as pictured, or optionally serve with a crisp green salad.

INGREDIENTS

2 pounds (908g) **fresh salmon**, skin and bones removed

1 inch (2.5cm) **fresh green ginger**, grated

¼ cup (59ml) **dark soy sauce**

2 tbsp. **rice wine vinegar**

1 **red chili pepper**, seeded and finely chopped (to taste)

2 tbsp. **powdered sugar substitute**

4 tsp. **sesame seeds**, toasted

NUTRITONAL FACTS
per serve

Calories 235, Fat 10.4g, Carbohydrate 5.1g, Dietary Fiber 0.4g, Net Carbs 4.7g, Protein 29.8g

SPICY CHILI PORK CHOPS

Yum! Juicy pork chops at their very best; heavenly with a green salad and an extra side of chopped avocado. These are also great cooked on a barbeque. Serve with seasonal vegetables of your choice.

Serves 6

DIRECTIONS

Mix together all of the ingredients except the pork chops and garnish in a small bowl.

Rub the chops with this mixture and leave covered in the fridge for a few hours for the flavors to develop.

Heat a griddle to medium high and griddle the pork chops for 7 – 8 minutes on each side until cooked right through but still juicy.

Serve garnished with lemon or orange slices.

INGREDIENTS

6 **pork loin chops**, about 6 ounces (170g) each

4 tsp. **powdered cumin**

2 tsp **powdered cayenne pepper** (to taste)

4 tsp. **dried marjoram**

6 cloves **garlic**, grated

2 tbsp. **olive oil**

Salt and pepper to season

Sliced **lemons or oranges** to garnish

NUTRITONAL FACTS
per serve

Calories 397, Fat 28.3g, Carbohydrate 4.8g, Dietary Fiber 0.8g, Net Carbs 4.0g, Protein 33.5g

KETO BOLOGNESE

Serves 6

A rich beef sauce to serve over spaghetti squash or Shiratake noodles.
Make a big batch as it freezes well and you will always have an extra meal on hand.
Shiratake noodles could be used to accompany this dish.

DIRECTIONS

Heat the oil in a large saucepan over a medium high heat.

Add the chopped onions and the garlic and sauté until the onions become translucent.

Add the bacon and fry until it begins to release its fat.

Add the ground beef and brown well, breaking up any pieces that may need it.

Add the rest of the ingredients except the cheese and mix well together.

Lower the heat and simmer for 1½ - 2 hours until rich and thick.

Serve hot with plenty of Parmesan cheese on top.

INGREDIENTS

1½ pounds (681g) **ground beef**

4 ounces (113g) **bacon**, chopped

1 **large onion**, finely chopped

4 cloves **garlic**, finely chopped

2 tbsp. **olive oil**

2 tbsp. **tomato paste**

½ cup (119ml) **dry red wine**

1 tsp. **powdered paprika**

1 tsp. **powdered coriander**

2 **bay leaves**

1 cup (237ml) **beef broth**

Salt and pepper to season

Parmesan cheese to serve

NUTRITONAL FACTS
per serve

Calories 452, Fat 32.2g, Carbohydrate 5.5g,
Dietary Fiber 0.9g, Net Carbs 4.6g, Protein 32.9g

CHICKEN & PECAN NUT STIR-FRY

A healthy, quick and easy to prepare way to serve chicken breast. The pecan nuts add a nice crunch and this could be easily changed for almonds or walnuts if you prefer.

INGREDIENTS

4 **plump chicken breasts**, boned and skinned

2 tbsp. **peanut oil**

1 inch (2.5cm) **fresh green ginger**, peeled and grated

1 **onion**, finely sliced

3 cloves **garlic**, finely chopped

6 ounces (170g) **brown mushrooms**, thinly sliced

6 ounces (170g) **broccoli florets**, chopped fairly small

1 **red bell pepper**, seeded and sliced

2 **small red chilies**, finely chopped (seeded for a milder flavor)

½ cup (119ml) **soy sauce**

1 tbsp. **granulated sugar substitute**

¾ cup (178ml) **water**

Salt and pepper to season

¾ cup (82g) **pecan nuts**, coarsely chopped

Serves 4

DIRECTIONS

Slice the chicken breast into small finger sized pieces.

Heat the oil in a large skillet or wok over a medium high heat and stir-fry the chicken for a minute.

Add the ginger and the onions. Stir.

Add the garlic, mushrooms and the broccoli and stir-fry for a couple of minutes more. The vegetables must remain crisp.

Add the bell pepper, chili, soy sauce, water and sugar substitute.

Stir well and cook for a minute more.

Season to taste.

Serve in bowls topped with the chopped pecans.

NUTRITONAL FACTS
per serve

Calories 452, Fat 22.8g, Carbohydrate 14.0g, Dietary Fiber 4.8g, Net Carbs 9.2g, Protein 46.8g

SPICY BEEF POT

Serves 6

DIRECTIONS

Heat the oil in a large saucepan over a medium high heat.

Add the onion and the garlic and sauté until the onion is translucent.

Add the beef to the pan and brown on all sides.

Add the curry powder and the chili and stir until fragrant.

Stir in the tomato, paste, bay leaves and broth.

Bring to the boil.

Turn the heat down to a simmer and simmer for 2 hours until the beef is tender and the sauce has thickened.

Check half way through the cooking time and add a little water if necessary.

NUTRITONAL FACTS

per serve

Calories 245, Fat 13.1g, Carbohydrate 5.5g, Dietary Fiber 1.3g, Net Carbs 4.2g, Protein 26.1g

Try this hearty, thick spicy stew. Serve hot sprinkled with cilantro if liked, extra chopped chili and some shredded cheese.
This dish would also work well in a slow cooker.

INGREDIENTS

1½ pounds (681g) **boneless beef shank**, cubed

1 **large onion**, finely chopped

4 cloves **garlic**, minced

1 **green chili**, seeded and chopped

2 **bay leaves**

1½ tsp. **curry powder**, mild and spicy

2 tbsp. **olive oil**

1½ cups (363g) chopped **tomato**

1 tbsp. **tomato paste**

1½ cups (356ml) **beef broth**

Salt and pepper to season

GREEK ROASTED LAMB

The aroma of lemon and fresh oregano will tempt you, as this lamb cooks to perfection in a slow oven. The roast is meltingly tender and falls apart. Serve with seasonal vegetables of your choice.

Serves 6

DIRECTIONS

Pre-heat the oven to 325°F (163°C).

Place the lamb in a large roasting tin.

Using a sharp knife, make insertions into the meat and 'stuff' each one with a garlic slice and a mint leaf; pushing both into the meat well.

Rub the meat with olive oil and then rub in the herb, lemon zest and seasoning to taste.

Place the lamb into the hot oven and roast for 4 – 4½ hours, basting with the juices every hour or so.

Check to see of the meat is done to your liking. If necessary turn the heat up to crisp the top. You may put it under a broiler.

Remove the meat from the oven and cover with foil.

Let it rest for 15 minutes before serve.

INGREDIENTS

1 x 4 pound (1.8kg) **leg of lamb** or 2 **shoulder roasts**, of similar weight

8 cloves **garlic**, peeled and sliced

4 **large sprigs fresh mint**, leaves only

3 tbsp. **fresh oregano**, finely chopped

2 **lemons**, zested

2 tbsp. **olive oil**

Salt and freshly ground black pepper

NUTRITONAL FACTS
per serve

Calories 589, Fat 36.4g, Carbohydrate 2.1g, Dietary Fiber 0.8g, Net Carbs 1.3g, Protein 59.8g

CREAMED CHICKEN WITH MUSHROOMS

Serves 8

DIRECTIONS

Melt 2 tbsp. butter in a large skillet (with lid) over a medium high heat.

Add the chicken breast and sauté until brown on all sides.

Pour over 1 cup (237ml) of chicken broth and cover the skillet.

Reduce the heat to a simmer and cook for 15 – 20 minutes until cooked through. Cook for a little longer if necessary.

Remove the chicken from the skillet and set aside.

Pour off the cooking liquid and set aside.

When the chicken is cool, chop into bite sized pieces.

Place the rest of the butter in a large clean skillet and heat over a medium high heat.

Sauté the carrot, celery, shallot and red bell pepper and the chili until tender.

Add the mushrooms and continue to sauté until the mushrooms turn a golden brown.

Stir in the remaining broth, the cooking liquid from the chicken and the cream.

Bring up to the boil and stir in the xanthan gum.

Season to taste with salt and pepper.

Stir in the cooked chicken and allow the dish to heat through completely before serve.

Serve sprinkled with chopped parsley.

NUTRITONAL FACTS
per serve

Calories 311, Fat 20.3g, Carbohydrate 5.0g, Dietary Fiber 1.9g, Net Carbs 3.1g, Protein 27.5g

INGREDIENTS

2 pounds (908g) **chicken breast**, skinned and boned

6 tbsp. **butter**

2 cups (474ml) **chicken broth**

1 **medium carrot**, peeled and diced

2 **stalks celery**, washed and finely sliced

1 **medium shallot**, diced

1 **small red bell pepper**, seeded and finely diced

1 **small red chili**, seeded and finely chopped

12 ounces (340g) **fresh button mushrooms**, quartered

1½ cups (355ml) **heavy cream**

2 tsp. **xanthan gum**

½ tbsp. **fresh parsley**, chopped

Salt and pepper to season

CHICKEN KORMA

A mild and creamy curry that originates from central and southern Asia; ideal for a Keto diet and very appetizing.
Serve sprinkled with toasted nibbed almonds and some cilantro.

Serves 8

INGREDIENTS

1½ pounds (681g) **chicken breast fillets**, skinned, cut into bite sizes

3 tbsp. **butter or ghee**

1 **large onion**, finely chopped

4 cloves **garlic**, finely chopped

1 inch (2.5cm) green **fresh ginger**, peeled and grated

¾ tsp. **powdered cinnamon**

1½ tbsp. **powdered coriander**

1 tsp. **powdered turmeric**

1½ tsp. **powdered cardamom**

2 tsp. **powdered paprika**

2 **red chilies**, seeded and chopped (to taste)

1¼ cups (120g) **ground almonds**

1½ cups (356ml) **plain Greek yogurt**

1 cup (237ml) **heavy cream**

1 cup (237ml) **coconut milk**

1 cup (237ml) **coconut cream**

3 tbsp. **tomato paste**

2 tbsp. **fresh lemon juice**

Salt and pepper to season

DIRECTIONS

Heat the butter, or ghee, in a large skillet (with lid), over a medium high heat.

Add the chicken and sauté until brown. Remove and set to the side.

In the same skillet, sauté the onion, garlic and green ginger until the onion becomes translucent.

Add all of the spices and chilies and stir-fry until fragrant.

Stir in the ground almonds, cream, yogurt, coconut milk, coconut cream and tomato paste.

Add the lemon juice and the chicken pieces.

Turn the heat down to simmer and cover with the lid.

Simmer for 20 – 25 minutes until the meat is tender.

Add some water if the korma is becoming too thick.

When the chicken is cooked, adjust the seasoning.

Serve.

NUTRITONAL FACTS
per serve

Calories 462, Fat 34.2g, Carbohydrate 13.6g, Dietary Fiber 4.8g, Net Carbs 8.8g, Protein 28.6g

SESAME SALMON KEBABS

Serves 6

DIRECTIONS

Make the citrus dressing by mixing together the sour cream, yogurt, ½ tbsp. lemon juice and some seasoning.

Cover and place in the refrigerator for the flavors to develop.

In a medium sized ceramic or glass bowl, mix together the rest of the lemon juice, lemon zest, chili, garlic, sesame oil and olive oil.

Add the salmon cubes and cover with plastic cling film. Place in the refrigerator to marinate for 30 minutes.

Remove the salmon from the fridge.

Thread the salmon pieces onto the skewers, alternating with pieces of bell pepper and zucchini.

Heat the broiler to medium high and broil the skewers for 6 – 8 minutes until cooked.

Turn the skewers at intervals during the broiling time to allow for even cooking.

Season with salt and pepper and serve with the citrus dressing.

NUTRITONAL FACTS
per serve

Calories 272, Fat 15.3g, Carbohydrate 9.8g, Dietary Fiber 2.2g, Net Carbs 7.6g, Protein 26.9g

Cook these under the broiler, over a griddle or outside on a summer evening over a barbeque.
Versatile and tasty served with a crisp green salad and a creamy citrus dressing.

INGREDIENTS

1½ pounds (681g) **thick salmon serves**, skinned and cubed

2 **medium lemons**, zested and juiced

1 **red chili**, seeded and finely chopped (to taste)

3 cloves **garlic**, finely chopped

3 **red or yellow bell peppers**, seeded and cut into large chunks

3 **zucchini**, cut into slices

1 tbsp. **olive oil**

2 tsp. **sesame oil**

½ cup (119ml) **sour cream**

½ cup (119ml) **plain Greek yogurt**

Salt and pepper to season

6 **kebab skewers**

BEEF & SAUSAGE CHILI

A very savory chili dish with the addition of bacon and eggplant instead of the more traditional beans. Serve with cauliflower or broccoli.
A sprinkling of shredded Cheddar cheese is also good.

Serves 6

DIRECTIONS

Heat the oil in a large skillet (with lid) over a medium high heat.

Add the bacon and fry until crisp.

Drain the bacon and leave to one side.

Add the onion and garlic to the skillet and sauté until the onion is translucent.

Add the chopped chili and the chili powder and cumin.

Add the ground beef and chorizo sausage and mix well together with the onion mix.

Stir fry until the meat is brown.

Add the tomatoes, eggplant, tomato paste and seasoning.

Return the bacon to the skillet and mix everything well together.

Cover and simmer on a low heat for 1 hour.

INGREDIENTS

1 pound (454g) **ground beef**

6 ounces (170g) **chorizo sausage**, ground

4 slices **bacon**, chopped

1 tbsp. **olive oil**

1 **large onion**, chopped

4 cloves **garlic**, finely chopped

1 **red chili**, seeded and chopped (to taste)

1 **large eggplant**, skinned and chopped

1 pound (454g) **fresh ripe tomatoes**, skinned and chopped

1 tbsp. **tomato paste**

2 tsp. **powdered chili** (to taste)

2 tsp. **powdered cumin**

Salt and pepper to season

NUTRITONAL FACTS
per serve

Calories 358, Fat 23.0g, Carbohydrate 13.4g, Dietary Fiber 5.3g, Net Carbs 8.1g, Protein 26.5g

MEATLOAF WITH A SWEET CHILI SAUCE

Serves 8

This is a family favorite, especially with children. Serve hot or cold. Meatloaf also makes a wonderful addition to a picnic meal.

DIRECTIONS

Pre-heat the oven to 375°F (191°C).

Grease a 2½ pound (1.15kg) loaf tin with a little olive oil.

Heat the rest of the oil in a large skillet over a medium high heat.

Add the onion and garlic and sauté until the onion is translucent.

In a large bowl mix all of the ingredients together, including the onion.

Place into the prepared loaf tin and cover with foil.

Cook in the hot oven for 1¼ - 1½ hours until cooked through and the juices run clear.

Remove from the oven and pour off any extra juices or leave to be reabsorbed into the meat loaf.

Cool for a while in the tin before turning out and serve.

Meanwhile place the vinegar, water, rice wine, garlic and chili in a small sauce pan and bring to the boil.

Boil until reduced by half.

Sprinkle in the gum and mix well.

Add the sugar drops.

Serve the sauce warm.

NUTRITONAL FACTS
per serve

Calories 441, Fat 31.7g, Carbohydrate 7.8g, Dietary Fiber 1.0g, Net Carbs 6.8g, Protein 30.7g

INGREDIENTS

1½ pounds (681g) **ground beef**

½ pound (227g) **pork sausage meat**

1½ cups (105g) **pork rind**, crushed

1 **large fresh egg**

½ cup (119ml) **tomato sauce**

1 tbsp. **fresh parsley**, chopped

1 tbsp. **fresh marjoram**, chopped

½ cup (57g) **mozzarella cheese**, shredded

¼ cup (25g) **Parmesan cheese**, grated

1 **large onion**, finely chopped

2 cloves **garlic**, finely chopped

1 tbsp. **olive oil**

Sauce:

¼ cup (59ml) **rice vinegar**

¼ cup (59ml) **water**

1 tbsp. **Japanese rice wine**

2 cloves **garlic**, minced

½ tbsp. **dried crushed chili flakes**

½ tsp. **xanthan gum**

5 drops **liquid stevia extract** (adjust to taste)

VEAL STROGANOFF

Delicate veal cooked in a luscious sauce of mushrooms and sour cream; this tastes truly amazing. Serve with broccoli spears and baby wilted spinach.

Serves 4

DIRECTIONS

Heat the oil and melt the butter in a large skillet over a medium high heat.

Add the veal strips and brown on all sides.

Remove and set aside.

Add the shallots and garlic and sauté until the shallots become soft and translucent.

Add the mushrooms and sauté for another few minutes.

Add the mustard, tomato paste, thyme, sour cream and seasoning.

Return the veal to the skillet.

Heat gently without boiling until piping hot.

When ready to serve, sprinkle the stroganoff with paprika.

INGREDIENTS

1¼ pounds (568g) **veal**, cut into thin strips

1 tbsp. **oil**

1 tbsp. **butter**

2 **shallots**, finely chopped

3 cloves **garlic**, very finely chopped

6 ounces (170g) **button mushrooms**, sliced

1 tbsp. **Dijon mustard**

1 tbsp. **tomato paste**

1 tsp. **fresh thyme**, chopped

¾ cup (178ml) **sour cream**

2 tsp. **powdered paprika**

Salt and pepper to season

NUTRITONAL FACTS
per serve

Calories 417, Fat 26.5g, Carbohydrate 6.5g, Dietary Fiber 1.2g, Net Carbs 5.3g, Protein 38.1g

PIZZA WITH PANACHE

Makes 16 Slices

Crispy cheesy crust, check! Tasty topping, check! Fantastic flavor!
That's three for three, enjoy! This recipe will make 2 pizzas.

DIRECTIONS

Pre heat the oven to 375°F (191°C).

Prepare 2 cookie sheets by lining with parchment.

Place all of the crust ingredients into a large bowl and mix together thoroughly.

Place half of the mixture in the center of each cookie sheet and spread each out into a circle using a damp straight edged knife.

The circles should be about a quarter of an inch (0.6cm) thick.

Place in the hot oven and bake for 25 – 30 minutes. Turn half way through the cooking time to brown on both sides.

Remove from the oven and set aside.

While the crust is cooking prepare all of the topping ingredients.

Heat the butter in a medium sized skillet over a medium high heat and sauté the onion and garlic until soft.

Spread the tomato sauce over the still warm pizza bases and top with the onion, bacon and cheeses.

Place under a hot broiler and broil until the cheese has melted and the pizza is hot 3 – 5 minutes.

Slice and serve topped with torn basil leaves.

INGREDIENTS

Crust:

16 ounces (454g) **mozzarella cheese**, shredded

3 **extra-large fresh eggs**, beaten

4 tbsp. **almond flour**

4 tbsp. **coconut flour**

1 tsp. **baking powder**

2 cloves **garlic**, grated

Salt and pepper to taste

Topping:

6 **slices bacon**, cooked until crispy and crumbled

1 **large onion**, finely diced

2 cloves **garlic**

2 tbsp. **butter**

1 cup (237ml) **tomato pasta sauce**

1½ cups (170g) **mozzarella cheese**, shredded

½ cup (57g) **Gruyere cheese**, shredded

Basil leaves, torn to serve

NUTRITONAL FACTS
per slice

Calories 226, Fat 15.7g, Carbohydrate 4.6g, Dietary Fiber 1.2g, Net Carbs 3.4g, Protein 15.8g

PORKERS & MASH

This sausages and mash dish with delicious sweet onions will delight the senses and appease your appetite.

NUTRITONAL FACTS
per serve

Calories 378, Fat 30.0g, Carbohydrate 13.1g, Dietary Fiber 4.7g, Net Carbs 8.4g, Protein 14.1g

INGREDIENTS

6 **pork sausages**, herby or spiced

2 **large onions**, finely sliced

1 tbsp. **olive oil**

3 tbsp. **butter** for sautéing

¾ cup (178ml) **vegetable stock**

¼ cup (59ml) **dry white wine**

¼ cup (60ml) **heavy cream**

1 **large head of cauliflower**, florets only

3 tbsp. **cream cheese**

2 tbsp. **butter**

4 ounces (113g) **Cheddar cheese**, shredded

Cayenne pepper to sprinkle

Salt and pepper to taste

Serves 6

DIRECTIONS

Heat a large skillet over a medium high heat and add the oil and butter.

Add the sliced onions.

Reduce the heat to medium low and sauté the onions until they are soft and have caramelized.

Meanwhile broil the sausages until nicely browned and cooked.

Add the sausages to the onions in the skillet.

Pour in the white wine and vegetable stock.

Turn the heat back up to medium high and simmer for a few minutes to reduce the stock by about half.

Season to taste.

Stir in the cream. Cover and keep warm. Do not boil.

Microwave or boil the cauliflower until very tender but not mushy.

Drain off any excess liquid and place the cauliflower into a processor or blender.

Add the butter and cream.

Process until smooth.

Season to taste and add the cheese.

Process again until the mixture is creamy and cheesy.

Serve immediately with the sausages in their onion sauce.

Sprinkle the mash with cayenne pepper for extra zing.

ARE YOU READY?
THE BEST BIT IS OVER THE PAGE!

KETO
DESSERTS

BUT FIRST
A NOTE ON DARK CHOCOLATE

In any recipes where dark chocolate is required, I've used a chocolate with 85% cocoa.
This is recommended to reduce overall carb content and of course, high GI sugars.

In general, be aware that the higher the cocoa %, the more savory the chocolate, so if desired,
adjust your sweetener to taste.

DESSERTS

PEANUT BUTTER FUDGE

Highly addictive! This delicious fudge is a must to keep in the fridge for that moment when something sweet becomes more than just a desire.

INGREDIENTS

1 cup (256g) **unsweetened smooth peanut butter**

8 ounces (227g) **butter**

4 ounces (113g) **full fat cream cheese**

¾ cup (150g) **powdered sugar substitute**

4 scoops **low carb vanilla whey protein**

1 tsp. **vanilla extract**

Makes 30 pieces

DIRECTIONS

Line an 8 x 10 inch (20 x 25cm) dish or pan with parchment paper.

Spoon the peanut butter into a saucepan and add the butter.

Melt over a medium low heat until the butter has melted and the peanut butter has softened.

Beat very well together.

Remove the saucepan from the heat and beat in the rest of the ingredients.

The mixture should be smooth with all the ingredients well incorporated.

Pour into the prepared pan and cool.

When cold, place in the refrigerator to set and chill.

Once set, cut into small pieces.

Store in the refrigerator in an airtight container.

NUTRITONAL FACTS
per piece

Calories 133, Fat 11.5g, Carbohydrate 1.5g, Dietary Fiber 0.8g, Net Carbs 0.7g, Protein 6.3g

NUTTY CHOCOLATE CUPS

Makes 20

These are like little fat bombs with a crunch from the chopped pecans. Keep them in the freezer and pop one into your mouth straight from the frozen state.

DIRECTIONS

Line 20 small muffin cups with paper cases.

Place the butter, peanut butter, chocolate and sugar substitute into a medium sized saucepan.

Melt everything together over a medium heat.

Beat well.

Remove from the heat and stir in the cream.

Stir through the chopped pecans.

Spoon the mixture evenly among the paper cases.

When cool, place in the freezer and freeze until firm.

Store in an airtight container in the freezer.

INGREDIENTS

8 ounces (227g) **butter**

⅔ cup (132g) **granulated sugar substitute**

3 ounces (85g) **dark chocolate**

2 tbsp. **heavy cream**

½ cup (129g) **unsweetened smooth peanut butter**

½ cup (55g) chopped **pecan nuts**

NUTRITONAL FACTS
per serve

Calories 186, Fat 18.1g, Carbohydrate 3.1g, Dietary Fiber 1.6g, Net Carbs 1.5g, Protein 3.5g

COCONUT CHOCOLATE SQUARES

Coconut and dark chocolate are staples on Keto and these zesty squares with a hint of lime are a symbiosis made in heaven.
Keep them in the fridge for a grab as you go sweet snack.

INGREDIENTS

Base:

3 cups (279g) **unsweetened coconut**, shredded

½ cup (119ml) **coconut oil**, softened

2 **small limes**, zested (and the juice from 1)

¼ cup (50g) **powdered sugar substitute**

Topping:

¼ cup (59ml) **coconut oil**, softened

6 ounces (170g) **dark chocolate**

¾ tsp. **liquid stevia extract** (adjust to taste)

Makes 16

DIRECTIONS

Prepare an 8 x 8 inch (20 x 20cm) mold by lining it with parchment paper.

Place the coconut, ½ cup (119ml) coconut oil, lime juice, zest and powdered sugar into a processor.

Pulse until the ingredients are well mixed.

Spoon into the prepared tin and place in the refrigerator or freezer for half an hour.

While the coconut layer is solidifying prepare the chocolate topping.

Melt the chocolate and the remaining coconut oil together in a ceramic bowl over a saucepan of simmering water.

Beat together well when melted and add the liquid sweetener.

Remove the coconut layer from the fridge or freezer and pour over the chocolate.

Place the coconut and chocolate mixture into the freezer.

Freeze for an hour.

Remove from the freezer and cut into 16 x 2 inch (5cm) squares.

Serve immediately or store in a covered container in the freezer.

NUTRITONAL FACTS
per square

Calories 214, Fat 20.8g, Carbohydrate 6.8g, Dietary Fiber 2.9g, Net Carbs 3.9g, Protein 1.9g

STRAWBERRY CHEESECAKE NIBBLES

Makes 12

These little dainty strawberry cheesecakes explode with flavor in your mouth – how delicious can Keto get?! Best. Diet. Ever.

DIRECTIONS

Pre-heat the oven to 325°F (163°C).

Prepare a 12 hole cupcake tin with paper cases.

In a small saucepan melt the butter, sugar substitute and stir until it dissolves.

Stir in the ground almonds.

Sprinkle a little of this mixture into the base of each cupcake case and press it down with the back of a teaspoon.

Bake these bases for 10 minutes in the hot oven. Remove from the oven and cool.

In a medium sized bowl, beat together the sugar substitute, the cream cheese and the almond extract.

Spoon this mixture evenly among the cupcake cases spooning out a hollow in the middle of each one.

Place the strawberries in a small saucepan and gently warm them until they begin to break up.

Cool the fruit and place a small spoonful into the center hollow of each cupcake case.

Place the cheesecakes into the pre-heated oven again and cook for 20 minutes.

Heat the chocolate and once melted, drizzle over the top of each one.

Remove from the oven and leave in the tin for 10 minutes.

Remove from the tin and cool.

NUTRITONAL FACTS
per nibble

Calories 229, Fat 21.8g, Carbohydrate 4.7g, Dietary Fiber 1.2g, Net Carbs 3.5g, Protein 4.4g

INGREDIENTS

Base:

2 ounces (57g) **butter**

2 ounces (57g) **ground almonds**

2 tbsp. **granulated sugar substitute**

Topping:

16 ounces (454g) **cream cheese**

¾ cup (150g) **granulated sugar substitute**

2 tsp. **almond extract**

½ cup (72g) **fresh strawberries**

2 ounces (57g) **dark chocolate**

CHOCOLATE CHEESECAKE

Arguably the most enjoyed of all the cheesecake recipes, chocolate.
Being so low carb and so tasty, it's really an amazing go-to Keto dessert.
Store any that may be left over in the fridge.

Serves 12

NUTRITONAL FACTS
per serve

Calories 480, Fat 45.6g,
Carbohydrate 8.8g, Dietary
Fiber 3.3g, Net Carbs 5.5g,
Protein 11.3g

INGREDIENTS

Base:

1¼ cups (120g) **almond flour**

¼ cup (28g) **flaxseed meal**

6 ounces (170g) **butter**

1 tbsp. **granulated sugar substitute**

1½ tbsp. **unsweetened cocoa**

Cake:

1 cup (200g) **granulated sugar substitute**

1½ pounds (681g) **full fat cream cheese**

¾ cup (178ml) **sour cream**

5 **medium fresh eggs**

2½ tbsp. **unsweetened cocoa powder**

1 tsp. **vanilla extract**

½ tsp. **xanthan gum**

Topping:

2 ounces (57g) **dark chocolate**, grated

DIRECTIONS

Pre-heat the oven to 375° F (191°C).

Prepare a 9 inch (23cm) spring form cake tin by lining it with parchment paper.

Place the almond flour, flaxseed meal, cocoa and one tablespoon of the granulated sweetener into a bowl.

Melt the butter and mix it into the almond flour mixture.

Press into the base of the prepared cake tin.

Place in the hot oven and bake for 20 minutes until pale brown.

Remove from the oven and set aside.

Lower the temperature in the oven to 325°F (163°C).

In a large bowl beat together the cream cheese with the remaining cup of sweetener.

Continue to beat as you add the eggs one at a time.

When the eggs are thoroughly incorporated, beat in the sour cream, cocoa, vanilla and the xanthan gum.

Pour the mixture on top of the baked crust and place it into the oven.

Bake for 50 – 60 minutes until the edges are well set but it is still a *little bit* wobbly in the center.

Turn off the oven and leave the cheesecake in it for another 20 minutes.

Remove the cheesecake from the oven and leave it to cool in the tin.

Refrigerate the cheesecake (still in the tin), overnight.

Just before you are ready to serve, remove the cheesecake from the tin.

Sprinkle the grated chocolate over the cheesecake.

Slice and enjoy.

CHOCOLATE PEPPERMINT MOUSSE

Serves 4

Make this choc-minty pudding in small individual glass serve bowls – it looks amazing and just invites you to dig in!
This is as close as it gets to an instant dessert.

DIRECTIONS

Have ready the glass serve bowls by chilling in the fridge.

Place all of the ingredients in a large bowl and beat very well for a couple of minutes until fluffy.

Spoon into the cold dishes.

Top with a dollop of whipped cream and serve.

INGREDIENTS

1⅓ cups (318ml) **heavy cream**, cold

¾ tsp. **liquid stevia extract** (adjust to taste)

½ tsp. **peppermint extract**

2 tbsp. **unsweetened cocoa**

2 ounces (57g) **dark chocolate**, grated

Extra heavy cream, whipped for topping

NUTRITONAL FACTS
per serve

Calories 292, Fat 28.2g, Carbohydrate 7.6g, Dietary Fiber 2.6g, Net Carbs 5.0g, Protein 3.4g

CHOCOLATE COCONUT FREEZE

This dessert is a little like an ice cream and is eaten straight from the freezer.

Serves 4

DIRECTIONS

In a medium sized saucepan gently heat the coconut cream and cream and stir in the cocoa powder. Do not let it boil.

Remove the pan from the heat and whisk well until the mixture cools.

Stir in the salt, vanilla and sugar substitute.

Whisk in the egg yolks.

Cool the mixture completely in the refrigerator.

Spoon the mixture into a freezer proof container and freeze for 30 – 40 minutes.

Alternatively, if you have an ice cream machine, after your mixture cools you may churn in the salt, vanilla, sweetener, and eggs and store in the freezer.

INGREDIENTS

2 cups (474ml) **coconut cream, full fat**

4 tbsp. **unsweetened cocoa powder**

¼ cup (60ml) **heavy cream**

2 **fresh eggs**, yolks only

1 tsp. **vanilla extract**

1 tsp. **liquid stevia extract** (adjust to taste)

Pinch of **salt**

NUTRITONAL FACTS
per serve

Calories 313, Fat 29.3g, Carbohydrate 8.9g, Dietary Fiber 1.8g, Net Carbs 7.1g, Protein 2.8g

CHOCOLATE NUT BROWNIES

Makes 9

Brownies are beloved for their gooey centers and rich chocolaty delights. These have some nuts in them for that extra layer of texture – enjoy.

DIRECTIONS

Pre-heat the oven to 375°F (191°C).

Line a 7 x 7 inch (18 x 18cm) baking tin with parchment and oil it lightly with a teaspoon of the oil.

Blend together the avocado flesh, half of the oil, eggs and the almond milk until very smooth.

Pour into a large bowl and fold in the flour, cocoa and baking powder.

Add the remaining oil and the liquid sugar substitute to the melted chocolate and mix it very well together.

Add the chocolate to the flour mixture and fold carefully together. Do not over mix.

Fold in the nuts.

Spoon into the prepared tin and place in the hot oven.

Bake for 25 – 30 minutes until firm. Do not overcook as brownies should be a bit chewy.

Remove from the oven and allow to cool in the tin for 15 minutes before turning out onto a wire rack to cool completely.

While the brownies are cooking make the icing by melting together the chocolate and the cream in a bowl set over simmering water.

Set aside to cool.

Whisk in the powdered sugar and the vanilla.

Ice the brownies.

Cut into squares with a hot sharp knife and serve.

INGREDIENTS

Cake:

1 **medium sized avocado**, peeled

½ cup (119ml) **olive oil**

2 **large fresh eggs**

¾ cup (178ml) **unsweetened almond milk**

½ cup (59g) **unsweetened cocoa powder**

2 tsp. **baking powder**

3½ ounces (99g) **almond flour**

3 ounces (85g) **dark chocolate**, melted

¼ cup (23g) **almonds**, chopped

½ tsp. **liquid stevia extract** (adjust to taste)

Icing:

3 ounces (85g) **dark chocolate**, melted

1 tsp. **vanilla extract**

¼ cup (50g) **powdered sugar substitute**

½ cup (118ml) **heavy cream**

NUTRITONAL FACTS
per brownie

Calories 391, Fat 36.0g, Carbohydrate 15.3g, Dietary Fiber 7.2g, Net Carbs 8.1g, Protein 7.6g

CINNAMON CREAM CUPS

Try this creamy soft dessert with a surprise crunch of pecans.

INGREDIENTS

3 cups (710ml) **heavy cream**

1½ tsp. **liquid stevia extract** (adjust to taste)

3 tsp. **powdered cinnamon**

2 tsp. **vanilla extract**

½ cup (55g) **toasted pecans**, chopped

DIRECTIONS

Pour the cream into a large bowl.

Add the spice, vanilla and liquid sweetener.

Whip the mixture very well until soft peaks form

Spoon into glass serve dishes and top with the toasted pecans.

NUTRITONAL FACTS
per serve

Calories 281, Fat 29.3g, Carbohydrate 3.3g, Dietary Fiber 1.1g, Net Carbs 2.2g, Protein 2.3g

GRANDMA'S EGG CUSTARD

Serves 6

A scrummy custard dish that is really awesome served with extra cream and berries too. It is however quite traditionally enjoyable on its own.

DIRECTIONS

Pre-heat the oven to 325°F (163°C).

Prepare a 5 – 6 cup ceramic or glass ovenproof dish by buttering it lightly.

Break the eggs into a large bowl and whisk until light and fluffy.

Add the sugar substitute, vanilla, salt and cream and mix everything well together.

Pour into the prepared dish.

Sprinkle the top with nutmeg.

Place the dish in a roasting tin filled with water – allow it to come 1½ inches (4cm) up the side of the custard dish.

Place the custard in the oven in the roasting pan.

Cook for 45 – 50 minutes until set and a knife inserted into the middle comes out clean.

Remove from the oven and the roasting dish.

Cool and serve.

INGREDIENTS

4 large fresh eggs

2½ cups (591ml) **heavy cream**

¾ cup (150g) **granulated sugar substitute**

1½ tsp. **vanilla extract**

¾ tsp. **salt**

Freshly grated **nutmeg**

Butter

NUTRITONAL FACTS
per serve

Calories 250, Fat 24.2g, Carbohydrate 3.0g, Dietary Fiber 0g, Net Carbs 3.0g, Protein 5.3g

KETO QUEEN OF PUDDINGS

Coconut custard with a crispy topping of meringue.
Serve with whipped cream and some crushed raspberries.

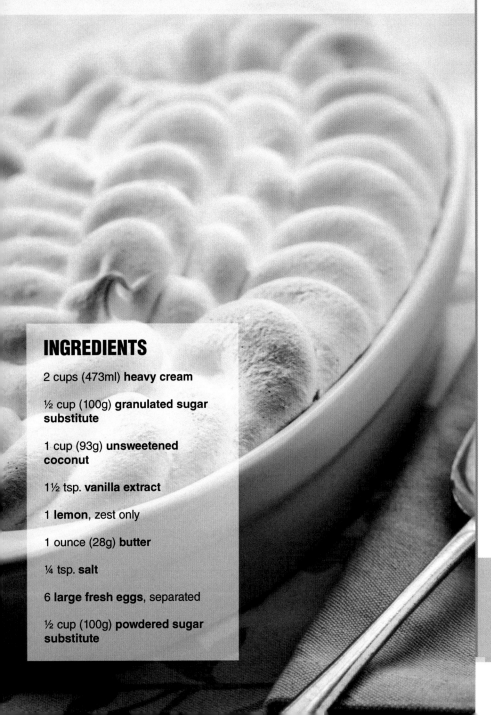

INGREDIENTS

2 cups (473ml) **heavy cream**

½ cup (100g) **granulated sugar substitute**

1 cup (93g) **unsweetened coconut**

1½ tsp. **vanilla extract**

1 **lemon**, zest only

1 ounce (28g) **butter**

¼ tsp. **salt**

6 **large fresh eggs**, separated

½ cup (100g) **powdered sugar substitute**

DIRECTIONS

In a large saucepan heat the cream, salt, and sugar substitute over a medium heat until just below boiling point.

Whisk the egg yolks to blend them and gradually pour over the hot cream mixture, beating all the time.

Pour this mixture back into the saucepan and place it on a medium low heat.

Stirring, bring the custard mixture back to a simmer and continue to heat it until it thickens and the custard coats the back of a spoon.

Remove the custard from the heat and stir in the butter, vanilla, lemon zest and the coconut.

Pour the mixture into a large ovenproof dish and leave to cool.

Heat the oven to 375°F (191°C).

Whisk the egg whites until soft peaks.

Gradually beat in the powdered sugar, a little at a time until a thick shiny meringue.

Spoon or pipe over the custard and place in the hot oven for 10 – 12 minutes until the meringue is crisp and brown.

Serve warm while the meringue is still crisp.

NUTRITONAL FACTS
per serve

Calories 301, Fat 28.0g, Carbohydrate 5.4g, Dietary Fiber 1.2g, Net Carbs 4.3g, Protein 7.6g

STRAWBERRY MOUSSE

Serves 6

DIRECTIONS

Mash or purée the strawberries in a large bowl.

Stir in the orange zest, orange juice and the salt.

Pour the purée into a saucepan set over a medium heat.

Stir in the strawberry jello powder and the sugar substitute.

Heat together until the sugar and jello powder has melted.

Remove from the heat and set to one side in a bowl to cool but not set.

When the strawberry mixture is cool, beat the cream separately in a bowl and fold it into the strawberries together with the vanilla extract.

Pour into a serve dish and place in the refrigerator to chill.

Serve decorated with freshly whipped cream and whole strawberries.

Strawberries and cream are a perfect combination for a light pudding to tingle your taste buds.

INGREDIENTS

10 ounces (284g) **fresh strawberries**, washed and hulled.

¾ cup (150g) **granulated sugar substitute**

1 **small orange**, juiced and zested

Pinch of **salt**

½ tsp. **vanilla extract**

2½ tsp. **unsweetened strawberry flavored jello powder**

1½ cups (355ml) **heavy cream**

Extra cream and fresh, whole strawberries to decorate

NUTRITONAL FACTS
per serve

Calories 147, Fat 13.0g, Carbohydrate 8.4g, Dietary Fiber 1.9g, Net Carbs 6.3g, Protein 1.3g

RASPBERRY CHOCOLATE CHEESECAKE

Luscious chocolate and raspberries combine sensationally in this enticing, rich cheesecake. I ate too many pieces last time I made this, just sayin... don't do as Ella does.

INGREDIENTS

Base:

4 cups (372g) **unsweetened desiccated coconut**

¾ cup (150g) **granulated sugar substitute**

3 **large fresh eggs**, whites only

4 ounces (113g) **butter**, melted

Filling:

1½ pounds (681g) **full fat cream cheese**

4 **large fresh eggs**

¾ cup (150g) **granulated sugar substitute**

4 ounces (113g) **dark chocolate**, melted

2 tsp. **vanilla extract**

½ cup (62g) **raspberries**

Topping:

½ cup (62g) **raspberries**

1 cup (237ml) **heavy cream**

NUTRITONAL FACTS
per serve

Calories 598, Fat 55.9g, Carbohydrate 14.5g, Dietary Fiber 6.5g, Net Carbs 8.0g, Protein 11.0g

Serves 12

DIRECTIONS

Pre-heat the oven to 350°F (177°C).

Line a 9 inch (23cm) spring form cake tin with parchment paper.

Mix together the desiccated coconut, melted butter and a ¾ cup (150g) of granulated sugar substitute.

Add the egg whites and mix again.

Spoon this mixture into the prepared tin and press it down with the back of a wooden spoon to form an even layer on the base and half way up the sides.

Place in the hot oven and bake for 15 – 20 minutes.

Remove from the oven and allow to cool completely.

While the coconut base is cooling, place the cream cheese in a large bowl and beat well to blend.

Add the rest of the sugar substitute, the melted chocolate and the vanilla essence.

Beat in the whole eggs one at a time ensuring that each one is fully incorporated before adding the next.

Squash half of the raspberries to give largish pieces rather than whole pieces of fruit.

Stir these through the cheese mixture.

Pour the mixture into the baked base and return to the hot oven.

Bake for 55 – 60 minutes. Bake for a little longer if still loose in the middle.

Remove from the oven and cool.

Chill in the refrigerator until ready to serve with the remaining raspberries and the heavy cream.

VANILLA CHEESECAKE

Serves 12

DIRECTIONS

Pre-heat the oven to 375°F (191°C).

Line an 8 inch (20cm) spring form cake tin with parchment.

Mix together the ground almonds, melted butter and cinnamon and press the mixture into the base and sides of the prepared tin.

Place in the oven and bake for 10 – 12 minutes until cooked.

Remove from the oven and cool.

Meanwhile prepare the filling by beating the cream cheese to soften it.

Add the eggs, one at a time, ensuring that each one is well incorporated before adding another.

Beat in the sugar substitute, salt, cream, lemon juice and vanilla extract.

Pour the filling into the baked crust.

Place the cheesecake in a large roasting tin filled with water to come 1½ inches (4cm) up the side of the spring form tin.

Place in the hot oven and cook for 50 – 60 minutes until set but still a little bit wobbly in the center.

Turn the oven off but leave the cheesecake in the oven for another 20 – 25 minutes.

Remove and leave to cool in the tin.

Refrigerate until chilled.

Remove the cheese cake from its tin and serve.

NUTRITONAL FACTS
per serve

Calories 424, Fat 39.3g, Carbohydrate 5.7g, Dietary Fiber 1.6g, Net Carbs 4.1g, Protein 11.4g

INGREDIENTS

Base:

1½ cups (144g) **finely ground almonds**

1 ounce (28g) **butter**, melted

½ tsp. **cinnamon**

Filling:

2 pounds (908g) **full fat cream cheese**

4 **large fresh eggs**

½ cup (100g) **granulated sugar substitute**

½ cup (118ml) **heavy cream**

1 tsp. **fresh lemon juice**

3 tbsp. **vanilla extract**

Pinch of **salt**

STRAWBERRY TART

Fresh like a summer day, perfect to complete your meal or just to serve with a cup of your favorite brew when you have time to put your feet up! Other berries can be easily substituted if you prefer.

Serves 8

INGREDIENTS

Tart:

7 ounces (198g) **almond flour**

2 **fresh eggs**

1 **fresh egg**, yolk only

1 ounce (28g) **butter**, melted

2 tbsp. **heavy cream**

½ tsp. **almond extract**

Filling:

1½ pounds (681g) **fresh strawberries**

½ cup (100g) **granulated sugar substitute**

½ cup (119ml) **water**

2 tbsp. **sugar free strawberry flavored gelatine**

Decoration:

Whipped heavy cream to decorate

NUTRITONAL FACTS

per serve

Calories 260, Fat 20.7g, Carbohydrate 12.1g, Dietary Fiber 4.8g, Net Carbs 7.3g, Protein 2.9g

DIRECTIONS

Pre-heat the oven to 350°F (177°C).

Butter a 9 inch (23cm) tart dish lightly.

Place the almond flour in a medium sized bowl and add the eggs, egg yolk, cream and almond extract.

Mix well together with a wooden spoon or your hands to make a dough.

Press the dough into the prepared tart dish and press as evenly as you can all the way around the sides and over the base.

Place in the hot oven and bake for 20 – 25 minutes until brown.

Remove from the oven and cool.

While the tart crust is cooling, hull the strawberries and cut them in half.

Place half of them in a small saucepan with the sweetener and the water.

Soak the gelatine if necessary in a little cold water.

Bring the strawberry mixture to the boil and simmer for about 5 minutes until the berries begin to soften and break up.

Add the gelatine to the hot liquid, stir well.

Remove from the heat and leave to cool for about 10 minutes.

Meanwhile arrange the rest of the strawberries in the cooled tart shell, cut side down.

Spoon the strawberry jelly mixture over the strawberries in the tart, being careful not to disarrange them.

Cool, and then set in the refrigerator for a few hours before serving.

Decorate with whipped cream.

DARK CHOCOLATE TARTS

Makes 12

Melt in the mouth fruity tarts you won't believe are Keto. These are soooo good. Just sensational in flavor and texture. For an extra treat, swirl with whipped cream on top and sprinkle with some grated dark chocolate.

DIRECTIONS

Pre-heat the oven to 350°F (177°C).

Prepare 12 hole tartlet or bun tin by buttering lightly with the 1 ounce (28g) of melted butter.

Place the almond flour in a medium sized bowl and rub in the remaining (unmelted) butter.

Add the egg, egg yolk, cream and vanilla extract.

Mix well together with a wooden spoon or your hands to make a dough.

Divide the dough into 12 and press a piece into each prepared tartlet or bun hole.

Press as evenly as you can all the way around the sides and over the base of each one.

Place in the hot oven and bake for 10 - 12 minutes until brown. Be careful they do not burn.

Remove from the oven and cool.

Melt the chocolate in a bowl over a saucepan of boiling water.

Cool the chocolate but do not let it set.

Beat in the powdered sugar substitute and the cream to make a ganache.

Divide the chocolate ganache among the 12 tartlet cases.

Pile the fresh fruit into the tartlets.

Serve immediately sprinkled with sugar substitute if liked.

NUTRITONAL FACTS
per tart

Calories 233, Fat 19.9g, Carbohydrate 8.4g, Dietary Fiber 3.6g, Net Carbs 4.8g, Protein 5.4g

INGREDIENTS

Tarts:

1 ounce (28g) **butter**, melted

5 ounces (142g) **almond flour**

1 **fresh egg**

1 **fresh egg**, yolk only

½ ounce (14g) **butter**

1 tbsp. **heavy cream**

½ tsp. **vanilla extract**

Filling:

6 ounces (170g) **dark chocolate**

½ cup (100g) **powdered sugar substitute**

4 tbsp. **heavy cream**

1 cup (130g) **fresh raspberries**

Powdered sugar substitute to decorate if liked

CHOCOLATE FLUFF TARTLETS

These decadent little morsels are a perfect sweet treat, super low in carbs, and absolutely bursting with taste.

INGREDIENTS

Bases:

3 ounces (85g) **almond flour**

½ ounce (14g) **unsweetened cocoa**

1 **fresh egg**

1 **fresh egg**, yolk only

½ tsp. **vanilla extract**

1 tbsp. **heavy cream**

½ ounce (14g) **butter**, melted

Filling:

4 ounces (113g) **butter**, softened

2 ounces (57g) **full fat cream cheese**

¾ cup (178ml) **heavy cream**

2 ounces (57g) **dark chocolate**

2 tbsp. **granulated sugar substitute**

Extra **cream** to decorate

Dark chocolate shavings to decorate

NUTRITONAL FACTS
per tartlet

Calories 255, Fat 25.1g, Carbohydrate 5.4g, Dietary Fiber 2.1g, Net Carbs 3.3g, Protein 4.0g

Makes 12

DIRECTIONS

Pre-heat the oven to 350°F (177°C).

Prepare 12 hole tartlet or bun tin by buttering lightly with melted butter.

Place the almond flour and cocoa in a medium sized bowl and add the egg, egg yolk, a tablespoon of cream and vanilla extract.

Mix well together with a wooden spoon or your hands to make a dough.

Divide the dough into 12 and press a piece into each prepared tartlet or bun hole.

Press as evenly as you can all the way around the sides and over the base of each one.

Place in the hot oven and bake for 10 - 12 minutes until cooked. Be careful they do not burn.

Remove from the oven and leave to cool completely.

Melt the chocolate in a bowl over a pan of hot water. Leave to cool but not solidify.

In a medium sized bowl, beat together the butter and granulated sweetener.

Beat in the melted chocolate.

Add the cream cheese and beat once more until a smooth consistency is obtained.

Whip the remaining cream into soft peaks and fold it into the chocolate cheese mixture.

Spoon or pipe the chocolate mixture into the baked tartlet cases.

Serve topped with extra cream and chocolate shavings.

NUTTY CREAM CHEESE DELIGHTS

Serves 8

DIRECTIONS

Place the walnuts in a food processor and pulse until they are like very coarse bread crumbs – do not pulverize.

Place the walnuts in a bowl.

Melt the chocolate in a bowl over a pan of hot water.

Cool slightly and then beat in the butter.

Mix this chocolate into the walnuts.

Make sure that the walnuts do not clump together but are coated in chocolate and remain as a crumble.

Place the peanut butter, cream cheese and sweetener into a bowl and beat well together until smooth and well mixed.

Have ready 8 individual glass serve dishes.

Place a couple of spoonfuls of the walnut crumble in the base of each one.

Top this with a spoonful or two of peanut cream.

Repeat these layers twice more.

Top each dessert with walnuts and berries and serve.

If you love nuts you will love this deliciously rich dessert. Layers of chocolate, walnuts crumbs and peanut butter cream – yummy.
You can reduce quantities and layers to decrease calories, that's up to you!

INGREDIENTS

12 ounces (340g) **smooth unsweetened peanut butter**

14 ounces (397g) **full fat cream cheese**

¾ cup (150g) **powdered sugar substitute**

2 cups (198g) **walnut halves**

4 ounces (113g) **dark chocolate**

2 ounces (57g) **butter**

A dozen **raspberries and strawberries** to garnish

NUTRITONAL FACTS
per serve

Calories 744, Fat 68.4g, Carbohydrate 19.4g, Dietary Fiber 6.7g, Net Carbs 12.7g, Protein 19.2g

ORANGE BUNS

Small individual cakes, that are popular with both adults and with children as a wonderful addition to a school lunch box for a tasty, guilt free citrus treat.

Makes 12

INGREDIENTS

4 ounces (113g) **butter**, softened

4 ounces (113g) **cream cheese**, softened

1 cup (200g) **granulated sugar substitute**

4 **extra-large fresh eggs**

1 tsp. **orange extract**

1 **large orange**, zest only

7 ounces (198g) **almond flour**

½ tsp **baking powder**

½ tsp. **baking soda**

Pinch of **salt**

DIRECTIONS

Preheat the oven to 375°F (191°C).

Have ready a 12 cup non-stick bun tray.

Mix together the almond flour, baking powder, baking soda and salt in a bowl and set aside.

Beat together the butter and the cream cheese.

Beat in the sugar substitute and continue beating until, light, fluffy and smooth.

Beat in the eggs one at a time adding a little of the flour mixture if it starts to curdle.

Fold in the rest of the flour together with the orange extract and the zest.

Spoon equally among the prepared bun cups.

Place in the hot oven to bake for 15 – 18 minutes until golden brown and springy when touched.

Remove from the oven and cool on a wire rack.

NUTRITONAL FACTS
per bun

Calories 235, Fat 20.9g, Carbohydrate 5.9g, Dietary Fiber 2.0g, Net Carbs 3.9g, Protein 6.9g

KETO CARROT CAKES

Serves 15

This delicious cake is so distinctive in flavor and easily cut into pieces
Made in a tray, it makes 15 small pieces.

DIRECTIONS

Pre-heat the oven to 350°F (177°C).

Grease a 9 x 13 inch (23 x 33cm) cake tin with butter.

Combine the flours, baking powder, baking soda, salt and spice in a large bowl and mix together well.

Melt the 4 ounces (113g) of the butter for the cake in a small pan.

In a separate bowl beat the eggs and sugar substitute until frothy.

Add the melted butter, almond milk and yogurt. Stir well together.

Mix the dry ingredients into the wet ingredients and combine well.

Add the carrot and the nuts and stir gently until they are well incorporated into the mixture.

Pour into the prepared baking tin and bake in the hot oven for 45 – 50 minutes.

The cake is ready when it is firm to the touch.

Leave to cool in the tin.

Meanwhile prepare the frosting by mixing together the remaining butter, cream cheese, powdered sugar and the vanilla extract.

Carefully spread this over the cooled cake.

Cut into slices and serve.

NUTRITONAL FACTS
per serve

Calories 374, Fat 31.6g, Carbohydrate 13.7g, Dietary Fiber 6.3g, Net Carbs 7.4g, Protein 6.9g

INGREDIENTS

Cake:

1½ cups (144g) **almond flour**

1¼ cups (140g) **coconut flour**

3 tsp. **baking powder**

2 tsp. **baking soda**

3 tsp. **powdered cinnamon**

½ tsp. **salt**

5 **large fresh eggs**

1¼ cups (250g) **granulated sugar substitute**

4 ounces (113g) **butter**

1 cup (237ml) **unsweetened almond milk**

¼ cup (59ml) **plain Greek yogurt**

1 pound (454g) **carrots**, peeled and grated

1 cup (117g) **walnuts**, chopped fairly finely

Frosting:

3 ounces (85g) **butter**

10 ounces (284g) **cream cheese**

1 tsp. **vanilla extract**

½ cup (100g) **powdered sugar substitute**

RED VELVET CUPCAKES

These popular, distinctive soft cupcakes, are divine topped with swirls of cream cheese frosting.

INGREDIENTS

Cupcakes:

¾ cup (84g) **coconut flour**

3 tbsp. **unsweetened cocoa powder**

½ tsp. **baking soda**

5 **large fresh eggs**

2 ounces (57g) **butter**

¾ cup (178ml) **unsweetened almond milk**

⅔ cup (132g) **granulated sugar substitute**

1 tsp. **vanilla extract**

2 tsp. **red food coloring**

Frosting:

14 ounces (397g) **cream cheese**

2 ounces (57g) **butter**

4 tbsp. **heavy cream**

1 cup (200g) **powdered sugar substitute**

DIRECTIONS

Pre-heat the oven to 350°F (177°C).

Line 12 muffin cups with paper cases.

Mix together the coconut flour, cocoa and baking soda.

Melt the butter and whisk it together with the eggs, granulated sugar substitute, vanilla and food coloring.

Fold in the dry ingredients together with the milk.

Spoon the mixture into the paper cases and place in the oven.

Bake for 20 – 23 minutes until risen and firm.

Remove from the oven and allow to cool for 5 minutes before placing on a wire rack to cool completely.

Make the frosting by beating together the butter, heavy cream, cream cheese and the powdered sugar substitute.

When it is smooth frost the cup cakes with a swirl of icing and serve.

NUTRITONAL FACTS
per cupcake

Calories 268, Fat 24.2g, Carbohydrate 7.5g, Dietary Fiber 3.0g, Net Carbs 4.5g, Protein 6.6g

CHOCOLATE DELIGHTS

Makes 12

DIRECTIONS

Prepare 12 muffin cups by lining them with paper cases.

Melt the 4 ounces (113g) of dark chocolate set aside for the bases in a small bowl over a pan of hot water.

Stir in the liquid sweetener and the nuts.

Divide the mixture up among the muffin cases.

Melt the remaining chocolate (as per the above method), together with the butter.

Remove from the heat and stir in the cream, vanilla extract and liquid sweetener.

In a separate bowl mix together the almond and coconut flour and stir them into the melted chocolate.

Spoon this mixture onto the chocolate layers in the paper cases.

Place in the refrigerator to harden.

Store in the freezer.

Decorate with the coconut before serving.

NUTRITONAL FACTS
per serve

Calories 325, Fat 26.9g, Carbohydrate 14.4g, Dietary Fiber 7.5g, Net Carbs 6.9g, Protein 5.6g

Take one chocolate nut base, and add a fudgy topping. Mix in a healthy appetite. Salivate, then enjoy! Keep these in the freezer in an air tight container for an anytime treat.

INGREDIENTS

Base:

4 ounces (113g) **dark chocolate**

¾ tsp. **liquid stevia extract** (adjust to taste)

3 ounces (85g) chopped **pecan nuts**

Topping:

¾ cup (178ml) **heavy cream**

4 ounces (113g) **dark chocolate**

2 ounces (57g) **butter**

1 tsp. **vanilla extract**

1½ cups (144g) **almond flour**

1 cup (112g) **coconut flour**

¾ tsp. **liquid stevia extract** (adjust to taste)

Unsweetened shredded coconut to decorate

LEMON BUTTER CAKES

These spicy lemon cupcakes smell so titillating as they are cooking you will be tempted to taste before they are iced. A small spoonful of sugar free lemon curd eats well with these cupcakes – place a little in the middle of the frosting.

Makes 12

DIRECTIONS

Pre-heat the oven into 375°F (191°C).

Line a 12 cup cupcake tin with paper cups or use a muffin tin.

In a bowl sift together the almond flour, baking powder and mixed spice.

In a large bowl beat together the butter and the granulated sugar substitute until it is light and fluffy.

Beat in the eggs one at a time, adding a tbsp. of the flour if the mixture begins to curdle.

Fold in the dry ingredients together with the almond milk, lemon zest and lemon extract.

Spoon the mixture into the prepared cupcake cases.

Place in the hot oven and bake for 15 – 18 minutes until firm and brown on the top.

Remove from the oven and cool on a wire rack.

While the cakes are cooling, beat together the cream cheese, powdered sugar substitute and the lemon juice.

Frost the cakes when they are cool by swirling a little frosting on the top of each.

INGREDIENTS

Cake:

2 cups (192g) **almond flour**, as fine as possible

⅔ cups (132g) **granulated sugar substitute**

5 ounces (142g) **butter**

¼ cup (59ml) **unsweetened almond milk**

4 **large fresh eggs**

2 tsp. **baking powder**

1 tsp. **lemon extract**

2 tsp. **powdered mixed spice**

1 **lemon**, zest only

Frosting:

1 cup (232g) **cream cheese**

2½ tbsp. **powdered sugar substitute**

1 tsp. **lemon juice**

NUTRITONAL FACTS
per cake

Calories 302, Fat 28.0g, Carbohydrate 5.2g, Dietary Fiber 2.0g, Net Carbs 3.2g, Protein 8.3g

CHOCOLATE BLUEBERRY NUT MUFFINS

Makes 18

This is the recipe that always gets people confused. Wait? These are Keto? But how? Fit for a king, these excellent muffins are a must to whip up for that extra special treat.

DIRECTIONS

Pre-heat the oven into 350°F (177°C).

Line 18 muffin cups with paper cases.

Crush the blueberries in a small bowl and set aside.

In a large bowl mix together the coconut flour, cocoa, nuts and baking powder.

Stir in the salt and granulated sugar substitute.

Melt the coconut oil.

Add the coconut oil, eggs, vanilla and heavy cream to the dry ingredients and beat well for a couple of minutes until everything is well mixed and the batter is thick and fluffy.

Carefully fold in the blueberries.

Spoon in to the prepared muffin cups.

Place in the hot oven and bake for 25 – 30 minutes.

Insert a toothpick into the cakes to ensure they are cooked.

Remove from the oven and allow to cool for 5 minutes before placing on a wire tray to cool completely.

While the muffins are cooling, beat together the cream cheese and the butter.

Beat in the powdered sugar substitute and cocoa.

Ice the muffins, top with a few blueberries, and serve.

INGREDIENTS

Muffins:

¾ cup (84g) **coconut flour**

¼ cup (29g) **unsweetened cocoa powder**

2½ tsp. **baking powder**

½ cup (59g) **walnuts**, finely chopped

½ tsp. **salt**

8 **large fresh eggs**, beaten

½ cup (100g) **granulated sugar substitute**

½ cup (119ml) **coconut oil**

3 tsp. **vanilla extract**

2½ cups (591ml) **heavy cream**

36 **fresh blueberries**

Icing:

8 ounces (227g) **cream cheese**

½ cup (59g) **unsweetened cocoa powder**

2 ounces (57g) **butter**

1 cup (200g) **powdered sugar substitute**

48 **fresh blueberries**

NUTRITONAL FACTS
per muffin

Calories 267, Fat 24.6g, Carbohydrate 8.1g, Dietary Fiber 3.4g, Net Carbs 4.7g, Protein 6.1g

NUTTY ICE CREAM LAYER

This vanilla ice cream combines with a chocolate crunch layer of toasty macadamias, and makes for a heavenly end to any meal.

NUTRITONAL FACTS
per serve

Calories 412, Fat 39.9g, Carbohydrate 9.9g, Dietary Fiber 3.3g, Net Carbs 6.6g, Protein 5.8g

INGREDIENTS

3 cups (710ml) **heavy cream**

1 cup (237ml) **unsweetened almond milk**

⅔ cup (132g) **granulated sugar substitute**

3 tsp. **vanilla extract**

5 **large eggs,** yolks only, beaten

1 tsp. **xanthan gum**

4 ounces (113g) **dark chocolate**

1 cup (113g) toasted **macadamia nuts,** chopped

Serves 8

DIRECTIONS

Prepare a cookie sheet by covering it with non-stick parchment paper.

Melt the chocolate in a bowl over a saucepan of hot water.

When melted, stir in the toasted macadamias.

Spread this mixture out onto the prepared cookie sheet and leave to cool.

When cool and the chocolate has set, break it up with a knife into small pieces and set aside.

Pour the cream, almond milk and the sugar substitute into a large saucepan over a medium heat.

Heat to just below boiling point.

Slowly add the hot cream to the beaten egg yolks, whisking all of the time.

When the cream and egg yolks are thoroughly mixed, return it to the sauce pan.

Bring the custard back to just under boiling, stirring all of the time.

When the custard begins to thicken remove from the heat and stir in the vanilla extract and xanthan gum.

Cool the mixture and then place in the refrigerator until cold.

Pour into an ice cream machine or place it into the freezer to freeze.

If using the freezer method stir the custard as it sets to avoid ice crystals forming.

When the ice cream is frozen layer it into a freezer proof container alternating a vanilla layer with a layer of chocolate macadamia crunch.

Place in the freezer.

Take the ice-cream out of the freezer 15 minutes before serve to soften a little.

CHOCOLATE CHIP COOKIES

Makes 24

DIRECTIONS

Pre-heat the oven to 350°F (177°C).

Line 2 large cookie sheets with parchment paper.

Mix together the almond flour, baking powder, mixed spice and sugar substitute in a large bowl.

Add the egg, milk and melted butter. Mix well.

Stir in the chocolate and the nuts.

Place spoonfuls of the mixture on the cookie sheets. Flatten slightly with the back of a fork. Add a pecan half on top of each one.

Place in the hot oven and bake for 20 minutes until golden brown.

Remove from the oven and lave to cool on the cookie sheets for 5 minutes.

Remove from the sheets and place on a wire rack to cool completely.

When cool, drizzle over some melted chocolate if liked.

NUTRITONAL FACTS
per cookie

Calories 161, Fat 15.3g, Carbohydrate 5.6g, Dietary Fiber 2.6g, Net Carbs 3.0g, Protein 4.0g

Be tempted with this scrumptious take on a classic cookie! Sugar free, buttery and full of nutty chocolate goodness.
Try other nuts such as macadamia for a variation. Store in an airtight container.

INGREDIENTS

2¼ cups (216g) **almond flour**

1½ tsp. **baking powder**

1 tsp. **powdered mixed spice**

4 ounces (113g) **dark chocolate**, coarsely chopped

¾ cup (82g) **pecans**, chopped

1 **extra-large fresh egg**

½ cup (100g) **granulated sugar substitute**

⅓ cup (79ml) **unsweetened almond milk**

3 ounces (85g) **butter**, melted

24 **pecan nut halves**

2 ounces (57g) **dark chocolate**, melted to decorate

NUTTY CHOCO BARK

Almost a fat bomb in execution, these are a real palate pleaser when trying to get that fat content nice and high, such as on a fat fast.
Indulge without guilt.

Makes 24 pieces

DIRECTIONS

Prepare a large cookie sheet by covering it with non-stick parchment paper.

Melt the chocolate together with the coconut oil and sugar substitute in a bowl placed over a saucepan of simmering water.

When the chocolate has melted, stir in the coconut and the nuts.

Spoon onto the parchment and spread the mixture out with the back of a spoon.

Place in the freezer to harden.

Remove from the freezer when set and break into 24 pieces.

Store in the freezer.

INGREDIENTS

6 ounces (170g) **dark chocolate**

1 cup (237ml) **coconut oil**

1 cup (113g) **macadamia nuts**, chopped

1 cup (93g) **shredded coconut**

½ cup (100g) **granulated sugar substitute**

NUTRITONAL FACTS
per piece

Calories 173, Fat 17.9g, Carbohydrate 4.2g, Dietary Fiber 1.7g, Net Carbs 2.5g, Protein 1.1g

STRAWBERRY SMOOTHIE

Serves 2

DIRECTIONS

Chop up the strawberries roughly and place them in a processor.

Add all of the other ingredients.

Process until smooth.

Pour into 2 glasses.

Enjoy.

Smooth, delicious and a wonderful creamy ending to any meal; this smoothie is certain to satisfy. Use strawberries instead of raspberries if you prefer, or even blackberries for a slightly lower carb count.

INGREDIENTS

1 cup (237ml) **coconut cream**, chilled

4 tbsp. **heavy cream**

1 cup (144g) **strawberries**

¼ tsp. **salt**

NUTRITONAL FACTS
per glass

Calories 339, Fat 32.1g, Carbohydrate 11.6g, Dietary Fiber 2.0g, Net Carbs 9.6g, Protein 2.4g

THANK YOU!

If you enjoyed these recipes, and I'm guessing your taste buds did, please keep an out for some of the other fun recipe books in the Keto Living Series, published by Visual Magic Produtcions and available from Amazon!

Thanks so much to my family, friends and the Keto community for keeping me loving all things Keto and making me smile every day.

Lastly, and most importantly, be good to each other!

Ella Coleman

Carbs Counted On Every Recipe

ELLA COLEMAN

Keto Living Cookbook: Lose Weight with 101 Delicious and Low Carb Ketogenic Recipes

The Keto Living Cookbook was written by Ella Coleman, an accomplished cook who loves experimenting with flavor combinations, and delights in eating and living a keto lifestyle.

It's no secret that carbs raise blood sugar, and our body produces insulin to get rid of it. The insulin then helps glucose convert to fat, and this is stored in our fat cells.

Goodbye self-esteem. Hello, cellulite!

On the ketogenic diet, carbs are limited and protein and fats are eaten in preference, keeping the body in a state of ketosis, and burning fats for a good, steady stream of energy.

The Keto Living Cookbook contains 101 recipes with easy-to-follow instructions for a scrumptious selection of meals and snacks straight from your kitchen to the table.

This book will be your constant kitchen companion with nutritional content, including a net carbohydrate, protein and fat count per serving listed for every single recipe. That's information you want, and need, right at your fingertips.

Lose the weight and love reaching your goals with the amazing selection of recipes to be discovered in the Keto Living Cookbook.

Carbs Counted On Every Recipe

ELLA COLEMAN

Keto Living Cookbook 2: Lose Weight with 101 Yummy & Low Carb Ketogenic Savory and Sweet Snacks (Volume 2)

The Keto Living Cookbook 2 is a tasty new offering in the Keto Living series from accomplished cook, Ella Coleman.

Containing 101 delicious, easy-to-make sweet and savory snacks, this exciting new collection of recipes dispels the myth that a life without carbs means a life without fun foods or flavor.

How can we have our cake, and eat it too? Staying low carb, and in ketosis is the key.

With a little fun and creativity, combined with the right ingredients and instruction, you'll soon be making mouth-watering Ketogenic masterpieces that are a pleasure to the palate and perfectly suited to your goals.

From pizza to pancakes, muffins to meatballs, ice-cream and more, the recipes you'll discover in the Keto Living Cookbook 2 are designed to satisfy a hunger yet leave you feeling curiously guilt free in the blissful aftermath.

Nutritional info with a net carbohydrate, protein and fat count per serving has been calculated for every single recipe, along with easy-to-follow instructions, plenty of variety and includes a detailed introduction on which lowest carb ingredients best replace sugar in a Keto recipe.

Carb & Fat % Counted On Every Recipe

ELLA COLEMAN

Keto Living – Fat Fast Cookbook: A Guide to Fasting for Weight Loss Including 50 Low Carb & High Fat Recipes

The Keto Living Fat Fast Cookbook is so much more than just a cookbook.

This unique outing in the Keto Living series from Ella Coleman, will take you on a journey into the exciting world of Fat Fasting, an excellent strategy to break through a stall in weight loss and guide you to a state of Nutritional Ketosis.

The Keto Living Fat Fast Cookbook starts by taking you back to the origins of Low Carb dieting and Fat Fasting and looks at the relevant pioneering studies and their astounding conclusions.

As the simple, yet effective protocol is examined further, important questions are posed.

What criteria qualifies as experiencing a weight loss stall, and are you a candidate for Fat Fasting?

What are the guidelines and safety considerations of a Fat Fast?

What is Nutritional Ketosis? Why does it matter and how can it be measured effectively?

And what kind of higher fat foods are most suited for a Fat Fast?

With questions such as these, and many more answered, the Keto Living Fat Fast Cookbook then delivers 50 delicious savory and sweet recipes, with all carbs and fat percentages measured, completing the comprehensive guide to this unique protocol.